MILL FAMILY

MILL FAMILY

The Labor System in the Southern Cotton Textile Industry, 1880–1915

Cathy L. McHugh

New York   Oxford
OXFORD UNIVERSITY PRESS
1988

Oxford University Press

Oxford   New York   Toronto
Delhi   Bombay   Calcutta   Madras   Karachi
Petaling   Jaya   Singapore   Hong Kong   Tokyo
Nairobi   Dar es Salaam   Cape Town
Melbourne   Auckland

and associated companies in
Beirut   Berlin   Ibadan   Nicosia

Library of Congress Cataloging-in-Publication Data

McHugh, Cathy.
    Mill family.

    Bibliography: p.
    Includes index.
    1. Cotton textile industry—Southern States—Employees
—History. 2. Cotton textile industry—Southern States—
History. 3. Family—Southern States—History. I. Title.
HD8039.T42U654   1988   331.7'67721'0975   87-7832
ISBN 0-19-504299-9

The views expressed are my own and do not reflect those of the Federal
Reserve Bank of New York or the Federal Reserve System.

9 8 7 6 5 4 3 2 1
Printed in the United States of America
on acid-free paper

Acknowledgments

I am indebted to the many people who have provided helpful suggestions and encouragement. Above all, I wish to express my deepest gratitude to three individuals. My interest in southern industrialization traces back to when I was a graduate student working as a research assistant for Gavin Wright. Gavin Wright has provided a source of inspiration and intellectual stimulation throughout this project. I have been fortunate to have benefited from his wise counsel. Paul David has always impressed me with the depth and range of his knowledge. His constructive criticisms and innovative suggestions have substantially improved the technical quality of my research. I am grateful also to Alexander Field for his painstaking reading and detailed comments on earlier versions of the manuscript.

Many scholars have provided invaluable guidance and useful criticisms. Special thanks to Jeremy Atack, Robert Gallman, Tom Kniesner, Tom Mroz, Barry Poulson, Gary Saxonhouse, Richard Sutch, Richard Sylla, Tom Terrill, Rachel Willis, and Robert Willis.

I have been aided by two unusually able research assistants, Sarah Duffy and Linda Hedberg. Finally, I wish to thank Sarah Mason for her patience and efficiency in typing this manuscript.

Preliminary versions of portions of this study have appeared in *Business and Economic History*, *Explorations in Economic History*, and *Journal of Social History*.[1] I am grateful to each of these journals for permission to incorporate some of the materials from those articles here.

New York City   C. M.
May 1987

Contents

Tables

MILL FAMILY

1

Introduction

The recruitment and utilization of a factory workforce for the southern cotton textile industry between 1880 and 1915 form the central subject of this book. Throughout the postbellum period, which saw the rise of a new cotton textile industry in the southern piedmont region, the labor force was composed mainly of members of families recently transferred to the mill villages from impoverished farms of the piedmont region. Both the source of factory labor and the patterns of labor organization differed from the earlier experience of textile firms in the northern states and created the basis for a distinctive social and economic structure—the southern cotton mill village. This book focuses chiefly upon the industrial developments in North Carolina and gives particular emphasis to the experience of the Alamance Mill as a representative case study. The internal logic and dynamics of the family labor system and of the form of mill village paternalism with which it came to be associated in the South are investigated and related to the problems encountered in securing a factory workforce in the southern piedmont region.

The new social history has been extended into the history of labor and the family. Recent research has stressed the significant influence exerted by culture, customs, and social institutions in shaping the labor process. According to Herbert Gutman,

> Men and women who sell their labor to an employer bring more to a
> new or changing work situation than their physical presence. What
> they bring to a factory depends, in good part, on their culture of
> origin, and how they behave is shaped by the interaction between
> that culture and the particular society in which they enter.[1]

Gutman has adopted a cultural approach to labor history, focus-
ing on the worker within the changing work environment. In
a complementary study of the relationship between the family
and social change, Tamara Hareven concluded that the family institution may provide a crucial influence in the process of
adjustment to industrial life.[2]

Within the traditions of social history and economic history,
this book provides a study of one historical experience, focus-
ing on the dynamic process of interaction and adaptation
between the southern cotton mills and the workers. Initially,
the character of the available labor supply predisposed the employers to adopt the family labor system and policies of mill
village paternalism; subsequently, the patterns of labor organization were influential in conditioning the worker to the factory environment. The patterns of labor deployment represented a response to the tensions confronting mill management
in recruiting and training a corps of factory workers and to the
tensions confronting mill families faced with the dramatic alteration in their social and economic lives as they migrated from
the farm sector to the cotton mill villages. The southern cotton mill village environment was neither a community created
entirely by mill management, nor was it a community created
entirely by the workers.

Cotton mills first appeared in the South during the late eigh-
teenth century, but their numbers did not increase rapidly. In
1790 a mill was established in South Carolina which harnessed
water power to "spinning machines, with 84 spindles each, and
several other useful implements for manufacturing every necessary article in cotton."[3] By 1826, apparently only four mills
were operating in South Carolina. While in the Spartanburg
area there were two prosperous factories at this time, the more
usual situation in the South appears to have been that of Mar-
ion district, where "labor is too valuable in raising cotton to be
devoted to manufacturing it into cloth."[4] The first cotton mill
in North Carolina was constructed near Lincolntown in about

1813.[5] The 1840s brought an impressive burst of activity in cotton mill production, but this wave of expansion ebbed quickly. The plantation slavery system, cotton cultivation, and dearth of sufficient white labor for mill work resulted in formidable competition for resources. Relatively few postbellum mills had pre-Civil War beginnings. Nevertheless, industrial-minded Southerners such as William Gregg continued to proclaim the potential profitability of a southern cotton textile industry that would concentrate on the production of coarse goods.[6]

Following the surge in cotton prices after the Civil War, the cotton market collapsed and prices tumbled through the 1870s. Total world supply of cotton was increasing as the growth in world demand for the commodity was slowing.[7] Subsequently, growth in the cotton manufacturing sector dramatically accelerated. Broadus Mitchell observed that from its historically uneven course of development, the industry had finally entered a sustained period of maturation and growth. He associated the year 1880 with the "genesis" of the southern cotton textile industry.[8]

The role of community-oriented activity and local subscriptions in supporting the creation of the new southern industry has received much attention. Momentum for the rapid rise of the industry derived from appeals to civic pride and Christian duty in sponsoring an industry that would create jobs for the poor whites and would help restore southern wealth and glory. According to Wilbur Cash, these appeals "acted upon the South of the time as the sermons of Peter the Hermit acted upon Europe of the eleventh century." The movement represented a "crusade preached with burning zeal from platform and pulpit and editorial cell."[9]

Quite independently of the humanitarian motivation for the "Cotton Mill Campaign" of the 1880s, the lure of profits undoubtedly provided a strong inducement for attracting investment funds to finance the mill boom after 1880. D. A. Tompkins, a major cotton textile manufacturer, estimated that the average net profit rate earned by the best North Carolina mills over two decades was 15 percent. According to Melton McLaurin: "profits of 15 percent and 20 percent on invested capital were not unusual during the 1870s." Further, the report on the textile industry in the 1900 *Census of Manufactures* concluded that "upon the whole the return upon investment in Southern cotton mills has greatly exceeded that upon factories in the North."[10]

During the early years, the capital necessary for financing the growth of the industry was predominantly raised locally. "Nothing stands out more prominently than that the Southern mills were conceived and brought into existence by Southerners."[11] Surplus funds were accumulated from local businessmen and planters through stock subscriptions. In correspondence during 1868, W. F. Leake sought financial support from close friends to rebuild a cotton mill situated adjacent to a 24-foot river fall. "I am about rebuilding my burnt cotton mill & for the want of means to accomplish so large an enterprize [sic] I propose to let others take stock in it. . . . If either of you have [sic] any surplus you wish to invest, I say as a friend, that this will be as safe and as good an investment as you can possibly make."[12] Subsequently he wrote to say that "The investment is perfectly good as well as perfectly safe."[13] In another case the owner of the Odell Manufacturing Company solicited investment funds from an employee to finance the expansion of his enterprise. The employee was tempted to subscribe because he thought that would serve to advance his career in management and he perceived it to be a lucrative prospect. "Notwithstanding the terribly dull year last year, the Mill declared a dividend of 11%, which is the lowest it has ever declared to my knowledge. I think that if it even does that well, it would be better than almost anything I know of."[14]

The direct flow of northern capital was delayed until long after the groundwork for a successful industry was firmly established. Northern assistance was not channeled directly through the banking community but through machinery manufacturers and commission houses. The manufacturers of machinery were often persuaded to accept payment in mill stock for 25 to 50 percent of the value of the machinery purchases. The machinery manufacturers generally wished to sell off the stock as soon as practical, as their main interest was only the completion of the sale of the equipment.

The commission houses or marketing agents played a crucial role in providing ready cash for working capital. With close banking connections, the commission houses obtained short-term credit which, in turn, they advanced to the mills against product inventory at a substantially higher interest rate. As the marketing agency for a mill's output, the commission houses levied a marketing charge. The latter normally was set at 4 percent of value on unbleached cloth and 5 percent of value on yarns and fancier cloths.[15] The commission houses also took stock subscriptions. Unlike the machinery manufacturers, the agents maintained a continuing interest in the mill operations and therefore tended to hold mill stock for a longer period of time.

Southern mills increasingly relied upon the marketing services of the commission houses, a trend one contemporary observer characterized as "slavery to the commission houses."[16] One mill that had sufficient circulating capital to maintain operations nevertheless reluctantly negotiated with a commission house for marketing services to avoid the risks and uncertainty of direct sales. "But how to avoid the middle or commission men and sell direct to consumers I don't know," bemoaned the mill spokesperson. "If there be any way to avoid it please don't hesitate to inform us."[17] By 1890 a survey of southern mills revealed that 65.6 percent of the mills contracted with New York agents. This reflects the extension of the market from the local region to the national level.[18]

In the early stages of the cotton mill boom, labor was generally plentiful. Whole families relocated from southern farms to mill villages. Parents and children obtained jobs together in the mills. With agriculture in decline during the late nineteenth century, the cotton mill was viewed as a haven from the depressed conditions of farming. Local destitute farmers turned desperately to the cotton textile mill as an alternative occupation. Farming productivity was low and not subject to improvement by hiring additional workers. This created a pool of low-paid and unemployed farm workers who could fill the expanding and contracting need for workers in the textile manufacturing sector during the 1890s. New entrants increased the total labor force by only 30 percent during that decade, but mill employment increased by 168 percent without generating substantial wage increases.[19]

The state of labor abundance was not to continue indefinitely. Relatively low wages had been influential in generating the rapid expansion of profitable mill operations. Eventually, however, the rising demand for labor was so strong that intense competitive pressure for workers resulted in labor scarcity and bidding up of wages after 1900, especially from 1905 to 1907. Not only were the number of establishments and scale of manufacturing increasing, but the demand for the products of the mills was strong. Cotton prices were also reviving from the depressed levels of the 1890s, substantially improving the employment prospects in the major alternative occupation, agriculture. Although the greatest wage pressure would likely have been exerted at the margin upon the wages of the recent entrants, the upward pressure would have had an impact upon the entire wage structure. Therefore, mill owners spent more on recruitment to moderate the steep advance in wages. In this way, they kept the wage differential required to reduce a given level of vacancies relatively low.

After 1900 the relatively passive role of the mills in securing operatives had given way to active recruitment efforts. Mill managers could no longer expect to meet their labor needs from local sources. They now had to reach out beyond the local area, even tapping labor supplies in the mountain regions. The mills engaged recruiting agents to persuade the mountain farmers to migrate to the mill villages, effectively increasing the industrial labor supply. "Whereas people had before straggled in at will, the mills now commenced concentrated efforts to get them out of the mountains."[20] In 1890 securing the capital to establish the plants presented a major difficulty; by 1907 the serious bottleneck had become insufficient labor, not capital. Nevertheless, in only rare cases were blacks employed, due to segregation policies.[21] Furthermore, foreign immigrants never accounted for a significant fraction of the labor force.

Although mill work was generally thought to be a more lucrative occupation than farming, the income of the head-of-household employed in the village mill was frequently considered insufficient to provide for the entire family. Supplementation of family income undoubtedly provided the major motivation of parents who sought mill employment for their children.

The composition of the labor force was also related to the pattern of technological innovation. With the introduction of ring spinning, skill and strength requirements for cotton spinning were relatively low. The weaving activities, however, demanded greater maturity, experience, and skill. Jobs were thus available for several members of a family as a group in the factory. The composition of the labor force by sex and age is provided in Table 1-1.

Cotton textile manufacture in the United States was concentrated in New England prior to 1880. During the following decades regional dominance gradually shifted to the South, especially to the piedmont region. This transformation is suggested by the differential growth rates of operating spindles, shown in Table 1-2, which reflect growth in productive capacity. In response to the challenge to her supremacy, the North shifted resources toward the production of finer grades of cloth. The pattern of specialization that emerged was dictated by regional comparative advantage. In the early years of the expansion boom, southern production was concentrated in the coarse grades of cloth which tended to have lower skill requirements. Eventually, with the acquisition of knowledge and experience by both management and the mill workers, the southern mills progressively upgraded the quality level of their output. From

Table 1-1. Composition of the Cotton Textile Labor Force, by Sex and Age: Percentage of Men, Women, and Children, 1880–1920 (Men and Women 16 and over, Children under 16)

Year	South[a]			North		
	Men	Women	Children	Men	Women	Children
1880	28.4	46.5	25.1	36.2	49.7	14.1
1890	34.4	41.4	24.2	43.3	49.8	6.9
1900	41.6	33.4	25.0	48.2	45.1	6.7
1909	52.8	29.5	17.8[b]	51.0	43.7	5.3
1914	55.7	29.7	14.5	52.8	43.5	3.7
1919	59.6	35.6	4.9	51.7	43.3	5.0

[a] Includes Alabama, Georgia, Kentucky, Mississippi, North Carolina, South Carolina, Tennessee, Texas, and Virginia.

[b] Due to rounding, percentages do not always total to 100.

Source: U.S. Bureau of the Census, *Twelfth Census* (1900), vol. 9, *Manufactures: Special Reports on Selected Industries*, pt. 3 (Washington, D.C.: Government Printing Office, 1902): 32; *Fourteenth Census* (1920), vol. 10, *Manufactures, 1919: Reports for Selected Industries* (Washington, D.C.: Government Printing Office, 1923): 161.

Table 1-2. Number of Active Spindles in Cotton Mills, by Region with Growth Rates: 1880–1900

Region	1880	1890	1900
Number of Active Spindles			
New England	8,632,087	10,836,155	12,850,987
Southern States	542,048	1,554,000	4,298,188
Decadal Growth Rates (in Percents)			
New England		25.5	18.6
Southern States		186.7	176.6

Source: U.S. Bureau of the Census, *Twelfth Census* (1900), vol. 9, *Manufactures: Special Reports on Selected Industries,* pt. 3 (Washington, D.C.: Government Pronting Office, 1902): 45–46.

1890 to 1900, the South led the North in the production of coarse cloth with the North experiencing an absolute decline in this product line between 1895 and 1900. The South overtook the North in output of medium grades during the following decade. It was not until after 1930 that the South was also dominant in the finest grades, as shown in Table 1-3.

Having considered some of the general history of the development of the southern cotton textile industry, let us look more closely at the story of an important cotton textile mill in North Carolina, the Alamance Mill in Alamance County. In one respect, this enterprise was unusual, for its roots lay in the antebellum era. The original Alamance Mill was founded in 1837 by Edwin Michael Holt and William Carrigan. Holt's father owned a grist mill that used water power from the Great Alamance Creek. After inspecting the Mt. Hecla Mill in Greensboro, Holt perceived a potentially profitable opportunity to harness the water power to the production of cotton textiles. Upon securing the promise of financial assistance, he ordered 528 spindles to establish a mill. Holt then entered into partnership with his brother-in-law Carrigan. Holt was responsible for management decisions concerning production and finance while Carrigan supervised bookkeeping and the company store operations.[22]

From 1845 to 1846 the scale of operations expanded with the purchase of an additional 528 spindles and the enlargement of the dam and water wheel. According to the entry on December 9,

Table 1-3. Regional Specialization of Cotton Goods Production: Quality of Output as a Percentage of Total Output, New England and the South

Year	Percentage of Total Pounds Produced in Each Region of Count:		
	20 or Less (Coarse)	21–40 (Medium)	41 or Higher (Fine)
New England			
1890	36.2	57.8	6.1[a]
1900	40.9	49.5	9.6
1909	33.5	53.2	13.2
1914	31.7	53.8	14.5
1919	28.9	58.0	13.1
South			
1890	94.0	6.0	—
1900	76.1	23.9	.2
1909[b]	61.4	35.0	3.6
1914[b]	53.2	44.7	2.1
1919[b]	58.5	38.3	3.2

[a] Due to rounding, percentages do not always total to 100.

[b] Includes Alabama, Arkansas, Georgia, Kentucky, Louisiana, Mississippi, North Carolina, South Carolina, Tennessee, Texas, and Virginia.

Source: U.S. Bureau of the Census, *Twelfth Census* (1900), vol. 9, *Manufactures: Special Reports on Selected Industries*, pt. 3 (Washington, D.C.: Government Printing Office, 1902): 42; *Fourteenth Census* (1920), vol. 10, *Manufactures, 1919: Reports for Selected Industries* (Washington, D.C.: Government Printing Office, 1923): 173.

1845, in the diary of Edwin Michael Holt, "Started new spining [*sic*] frame—performed well."[23] Weaving operations were successfully integrated into the mill in 1848. The start of weaving activity, initially planned for late 1847, had been delayed by the late arrival of equipment. A letter in October of that year stated, "Our looms have not come to hand yet neither have we heard from [the equipment suppliers] tho [*sic*] the time is out more than a month that they were to have been shipped."[24] Describing the success of the weaving venture, Alfred A. Holt wrote in 1849: "We have 12 looms in operation & are turning of some as good 4/4 sheetings as you ever saw, which we sell at 7¢ per yard. We are also making a 7/8 goods for 6¢ per yard all of which we sell as fast as we make, the 7/8 goods is out.

There is not a yard in the house at present & but very little of the 4/4."[25]

During the antebellum period, men, women, and children were employed by the Alamance Mill. Edwin Holt included references to male workers in his diary: "Started Eli Albright to Hillsboro with a load of yarn" and "Hired boy Harvey of Mrs. Frieland at 50 dollars for the year."[26] A writer in 1860 commented upon the employment of females in the Alamance Mill: "I went in [the mill], and was pleased to see the hands of intelligent white females employed in a useful occupation. . . . This mill . . . gives employment and comfort to many poor girls who might otherwise be wretched."[27]

In 1853 on-site dyeing, a finishing process, was introduced that would firmly establish the reputation and success of the Alamance Mill. An unemployed, experienced French dyer agreed to instruct Edwin Holt's son in the art of dyeing. The final product, the Alamance plaid, was the first colored cotton cloth woven on power looms in the South. The plaids were the mainstay of Alamance County production until about 1900 when output was shifted to ginghams.

The Alamance Mill had distributed goods through a retail general store during the antebellum period. Following the introduction of weaving, emphasis shifted to sales to wholesale grocers who then sold the plaids to general stores. Another peculiar feature of the enterprise was that the Alamance Mill lagged behind the rest of the South during the 1880s in the employment of the services of the northern agents. In 1902 when contacted by Walter F. Carlile, a Philadelphia commission house, the Alamance Mill steadfastly maintained its independence from the commission system and declined the services offered: "Replying to your favor . . . we have nothing to offer, as our product is all sold direct and do nothing with Commission houses. With thanks to you, We remain, Yours very truly."[28] However, by 1920, all the mills in Alamance County were employing marketing agents.

Cotton textile production in Alamance County was largely a Holt family venture. Substantial assistance in mill operations was provided by Edwin Holt's sons, son-in-law, and grandsons. His older brother, William Holt, a successful planter, supplied local short staple cotton used in the mill as well as financial capital for mill expansion. The family enterprise survived both the retirement of Edwin Holt in 1866 and the destruction of the original factory by fire in 1872. The old mill was replaced by one outfitted with the most modern equipment. Over the years the capacity of the new factory increased. In 1886 it had 1,200 spindles and 94 looms, and by 1905, 2,500 spindles and 120 looms. The family textile operations also expanded by acquiring more mills. In 1880 four of the six mills operating in Alamance County were controlled by the Holts. Three of four plants then under construction were also Holt family enterprises. The unusual pattern of dominance was to continue during the next 40 years. By 1919, the Holt family controlled 23 of 27 textile mills in the county, 78 percent of the spindles, and 83 percent of the looms in Alamance County.[29]

The following chapters analyze the process whereby a growing industry was able to attract and develop a labor force recruited from the farm community. The internal logic and rationale for the system of labor organization is established. From a study of the creation of the textile factory workforce in India, Morris Morris concluded "that the creation of a disciplined industrial labor force in a newly developing society is not particularly difficult." He further maintained that, to a large extent, the employer in India unilaterally determined the pattern of labor organization: "The necessities imposed by industrial technology and markets required employers to select different systems of discipline, and these determined the way labor would work." Moreover,

> it seems safe to conclude that the labor problems with which the industry had to contend did not flow primarily from the psychology of the work force or from the rigid traditions and structure of the rural social order. Such instability and indiscipline as did exist stemmed from the character of employer policies which were determined by the economic and technical characteristics of the enterprises . . . . at least until the 1920's the industry got precisely the kind of labor force and the kind of labor discipline that it wanted and needed.[30]

The conclusions presented in this book are at variance with Morris' findings for the Indian industry. The development of the southern mill workforce involved a complex interrelationship and process of adjustment between the mill and the workers. This interaction represented a resolution to the challenges introduced by the shift from the household farm to the mill village and factory setting.

This book fills a void in the history of American labor. Until recently, most studies of the linkages between labor supply and industrialization have focused primarily on the technological transformation of the economy.[31] However, in the spirit of the new social history, this research stresses the importance of institutions and culture as well as technological change in analyzing industrial labor conditions. This book does not examine the issue of labor conditions during the transition to industrialization in general; rather, it is based on the labor conditions of a particular industrial experience, the growth of the southern cotton textile industry during the postbellum period. This is a study of the dynamic process of response and interaction between the southern cotton mill workers and mill managers. Also, at a broader level of inquiry, this is a study of a particular form of labor organization, the family labor system.

To secure a labor force, mill managers formulated policies to meet the dual personnel functions of initial recruitment of workers and the continuing employee development programs for current mill village residents. Mill managers adopted the family labor system, a system in which several members of the household, including children, were employed as operatives. The organization of labor based upon the family unit represented an important unifying element in the labor process as a whole.

Although initially the mill village was constructed to gather together a workforce, it gradually emerged as an instrument to control the workers. Management was forced to find the means to develop worker discipline in a novice factory workforce. The mill village became the focal point of economic and social cohesion, as well as an institution for socializing and stabilizing the workforce. Company paternalism exercised a dominating influence in the mill communities.

Chapter 2 provides an introduction to the mill village environment and examines the difficulties associated with labor recruitment, retention, and discipline. The analysis relies heavily on a heretofore unexploited source of primary data, the records of the Alamance Mill. The mill records include the daily payroll books, the company store ledgers, the rental housing accounts, personal diaries, and business correspondence. (A description of these records and the preparation of the data set is provided in Appendix A.) This chapter, which focuses primarily upon an individual mill as a case study, serves also as an initial frame of reference for subsequent chapters which discuss the varied dimensions of the labor process in the southern piedmont cotton textile industry.

Further, Chapter 2 reports the results of an econometric study of the major determinants of individual earnings in the Alamance Mill. Earnings functions are estimated for each of the 23 years between 1890 and 1912. The set of independent variables includes experience, sex, age, and literacy. The analysis reveals that experience and sex were important determinants but that age and education were not significant factors in explaining individual earnings. In many respects, the structure of cotton mill wages and the terms of employment were designed to foster the emergence of an experienced, stable workforce.

Although experience exerted a significant positive influence on earnings, its contribution declined over time. This may perhaps be attributed to a changing wage structure as the industry matured, with no change in individual persistence rates. Smaller premiums would be paid to experienced workers as the core group of tenured workers expanded over time. Alternatively, the shift in the wage structure may have reflected the increasing strength of the attachment of the family to the mill due to the stabilizing influence of the family labor system and mill village paternalism.

The analysis indicates that sex wage differentials persisted even when payments were based on uniform piece rates, suggesting the existence of real productivity differences. Nevertheless, there is also evidence of sexual discrimination in the labor market.

Economic exigency and social custom explain parental pressure for child labor, but a fundamental explanation or rationale for the reliance of the mills upon child labor is more complex. Chapter 3 examines the role of child labor as an integral component of the family labor system. The paradox of the simultaneous pressure for both continuation and elimination of the practice of child labor is resolved with reference to the operation of the internal job market and labor bargaining process. Both parties, the managers and the mill operatives, influenced the outcome of the job bargaining process. By hiring labor in family units, the mill managers were able to attract the mature primary workers as well as the complementary casual workers for relatively low wages.

In view of the surprising results obtained in Chapter 2 concerning the effect of education on individual wages, it is important to seek the rationale for the financial support of schools by mill companies. Chapter 4, therefore, analyzes the motivations for schooling and the supply and demand for literate workers. The provision of schooling is related to two fundamental personnel functions: recruitment and development of a disciplined workforce. Schools served initially to attract high-quality workers by offering education for their children. In the absence of a comprehensive public educational system, mill schools were important in assuring a continuing supply of literate workers to the mill. Furthermore, mill owners believed the schools to be effective instruments for inculcating acceptable patterns of behavior among the young workers. Finally, the establishment of schools provided the mills additional leverage during job negotiations with family units.

Demographers have observed that family size in industrial centers frequently tends to be smaller than in agrarian regions. In contrast, the cotton mill villages tended to gather together relatively large families in the factory community. Chapter 5 attempts to explain the economic motivation for observed patterns of fertility behavior, family size, marital age, and labor force participation within the mill village. Family decisions were strongly influenced by the value of property rights vested in the labor services of children. Although the family labor system tended to preserve family cohesion when the family moved from farm to factory, the family labor system in turn exerted an influence upon the family unit itself.

Finally, Chapter 6 compares the family labor system with systems of labor organization that emerged under different settings. At a similar stage of industrial development, the mills in Lowell, Massachusetts, employed a predominantly young, single female workforce housed in dormitories. Furthermore, Japanese mills in the late nineteenth and early twentieth centuries also employed mostly young women as mill operatives. Comparisons of the three systems illuminate the unique southern conditions that supported or fostered the establishment of the family labor system.

A comparison of the foundations of different labor systems reveals the historical forces or influences that led to the adoption of a particular form of labor organization, the family labor system. Certain patterns or regularities are discerned that would be considered characteristic of conditions conducive to the emergence of a family labor system, independent of the specific geographical or chronological setting.

2

The Terms of Employment

Because the South was predominantly an agricultural region after the Civil War, it lacked a large pool of experienced industrial wage laborers. Therefore the rapid growth of the southern cotton textile operations during the postbellum period was supported by a migration of the population from agrarian pursuits to the manufacturing sector. The labor shift was accomplished largely by a transfer of entire family units from the farm to the mill village.

Reliance upon an inexperienced industrial workforce presented difficult challenges for the textile manufacturers. The adoption of the family labor system was predicated upon the composition and attributes of the mill workforce. Thus the quality and character of the available pool of workers tended to shape the form of labor organization that was initially adopted. The terms of employment encompassed the entire configuration of working conditions, including wages, joint job offers to several members of the family, seniority privileges, promotion possibilities, and the company-sponsored employee welfare program. In the postbellum southern cotton textile industry, the terms of employment were structured to promote the development of a stable, experienced workforce.

The mill village evolved as the center of economic and social activities, as well as an institution for socializing, stabilizing, and controlling the workforce. As mills were frequently located near the river fall line away from major population centers, mills provided subsidized housing in the mill village to attract the families.

The employment of a novice factory workforce introduced tensions in the labor process. The paternalistic development of the comprehensive welfare system was a response to the type of workers attracted to the mill villages. Welfare activities, including moral guidance, church sponsorship, company housing, the company store, entertainment, and education, exerted a pervasive influence over the lives of the workers.

Mill paternalism was viewed as a strategy for developing a disciplined workforce. Although the humanitarian motive cannot be dismissed, the comprehensive welfare program was consistent with mill owners' efforts to maximize profits. One mill president observed: "Some mill management believe that it pays a corporation to make reasonable expenditures to produce a higher class of operatives loyal to the corporation, and that best results in the long run for the corporation are so obtained."[1] Hence, resources devoted to the paternalistic welfare activities were justified as an investment in the improvement of the quality of the workforce.

Many cotton mills depended upon water power and were therefore situated in remote areas near the fall line of a river or stream. The firms constructed homes for the families who moved to the mill villages seeking employment. In addition, by providing subsidized housing the firms conserved on precious working capital; subsidized housing allowed for a lower total wage bill and lower circulating cash requirements. The ownership of the village houses and the consequent power of eviction provided the firm an instrument of control over the workers. After a mill was ordered reopened following a smallpox scare, 40 frightened workers refused to return to work. The manager wrote about the incident in a personal letter:

> I heard of it right away, and gave them fifteen minutes to get back into the Mill, and also told the parents that if they didn't send their children in the Mill immediately, that they would have to vacate our houses at once. All came back in time, & I let them all go to work except the one that started the bolt—I discharged him & have made him get out of the company's house.[2]

The general rule in North Carolina required that a family occupying a company dwelling provide one operative for each room of the house or sometimes two operatives for a three-room house. The rent charged workers of the Alamance Mill ranged from 35 cents to 60 cents per week and remained stable from 1908 to 1920. The 24 company houses each had from four to six rooms. Many families took in boarders to help meet both the rental payment and the mill requirement that there be a minimum number of workers in the home. Included within a 1900 sample of 348 Alamance County cotton textile workers were 26 individuals identified as boarders, three of whom worked in the Alamance Mill.[3]

Company stores offered general merchandise such as groceries, dry goods, and home necessities. The company stores may have been established to counteract private retail monopoly power. Alternatively, private retailers may have been hesitant to establish outlets in isolated areas. It was claimed that the early stores exacted exorbitant prices for the wares, but by 1906, their prices tended to be 5 to 10 percent lower than elsewhere. The stores also served to conserve on the circulating cash requirements of the firm. The stores often maintained wage accounts, and the mills subtracted credit purchases before distributing wages. The company stores facilitated the introduction of scrip payment to workers, redeemable for store purchases or cash at the end of a month. One mill official commented, "We would settle with the cash all the time if we had a bank convenient to us, but to pay weekly in cash would require an extra hand on the road most of his time to keep a supply of money on hand."[4] Workers at some mills, including at least one mill in Alamance County, were expected, as a condition of employment, to shop at the company store. Furthermore, other merchants in the community often accepted the mill scrip only at a substantial discount.[5]

The mill management undertook to provide moral guidance as part of the socialization process of mill families. Managers attempted to establish standards or patterns of acceptable behavior for a group of workers who were frequently thought to be ignorant, unstable, impractical, and ill-mannered. "Sometimes the people brought with them little besides bad habits and a total dependence upon the management for moral care and physical upbuilding."[6] Management hoped to promote the acceptance of social norms that would foster the development of worker discipline. Mill managers frequently held official positions in the company church, setting an example of religious piety and servitude. A mill official in Cleveland County in 1891 reported, "Two of the stockholders, the President and Treasurer, teach in the Sabbath school."[7] Immoral behavior was not tolerated. The use of snuff and alcohol was officially frowned upon due to the industrial hazards posed by the consumption of these substances. One manager claimed, "Ninety percent of the operatives—kids and all—used to use snuff. We would get from the loom-boxes, where they would leave them, a barrel of snuff boxes a week in cleaning. Now not fifteen per cent use snuff."[8] Nonetheless, entries in the accounts of the Alamance Mill company store ledgers indicate that workers at the Alamance Mill made tobacco purchases.

Another important dimension of the paternalistic relationship between the factory and the worker was the provision of schooling. Frequently the mills supported formal schooling far beyond the local property tax requirement. Education was advocated by mill management for its contribution to productivity, especially as output progressively tended toward finer quality levels. Schools fostered literacy and the development of desirable worker traits. Furthermore, the provision of superior school facilities was offered as an inducement to attract the most productive workers from the pool of job applicants. Thus, schools served a role in both the initial recruitment of workers and the on-going training programs. An alternative interpretation was advanced by David Carlton. He contends that a major factor in the decision to provide school facilities was the benefit to be derived in public relations.[9]

A Senate investigative study of 152 southern mills in 1907 reported that 51.3 percent of the mills wholly or partially financed schools for mill village children. The county district school near the Alamance Mill offered a regular two-month term or a three-month term available by private subscription. The sons and grandsons of the founder of the Alamance Mill attended here as well as the mill children.[10] From the sample of 348 textile workers in Alamance County in 1900, 7 workers attended school sometime during the preceding year, 31 could neither read nor write, 5 could read but not write, and the remainder (305) could both read and write. Among cotton mill operatives in Alamance County in 1903, 91 percent of the adults and 86 percent of the children were literate.[11]

The acquisition of skill depended upon accumulated experience as well as education. It was well-known that it took greater skill to produce the finer grades of cloth than to produce the coarse grades. An unskilled labor force effectively precluded the possibility of producing the finer grades. Simpson Bobo Tanner, a mill owner, had a deep desire to produce fine quality cloth but after assessing the situation critically, "his yearning never overcame his common sense."[12]

If the mill managers were able to attract and retain some workers who would remain employed by a firm for many years, this would facilitate the shift in production toward higher quality output. In addition, high turnover rates tend to lower productivity and efficiency in the factory. Firms incur greater hiring and training costs as turnover increases.

Accounts of the mobility or shiftlessness of southern workers are numerous. A Senate document reported that

> The cotton-mill hands in the South are an extremely independent set of people who do not hesitate, upon a slight provocation or from a pure whim, to leave one mill and go to another. . . . In 91 mills, with a total regular pay roll of 28,893, [in 1907] the *estimated* annual pay roll was 50,786 hands, thus showing that for every 100 hands on the regular roll an *estimated* change of 75 hands takes place during the year.[13]

However, a close examination of the employment histories of Alamance Mill workers reveals extensive individual variation in turnover rates. Reliance on aggregate data only and the failure to track the individual records have perhaps caused misleading conclusions to be drawn in the past regarding worker reliability. Furthermore the quit rate was strongly influenced by the hiring policies of the mills themselves. During the period of labor shortage, individual mills resorted to "raiding" or luring workers away from competing mills. This recruitment practice was publicly condemned by many mills, although unilateral efforts to abolish the practice were considered futile and costly.

> The employees of cotton mills, generally, are too migratory. . . . The mill managers are to blame for this by too much enticing, and many times offering inducements that they cannot live up to. If this one

Table 2-1. Average Experience, Alamance Mill Operatives

| Mean Experience | | Mean Experience | |
Year	(Years)[a]	Year	(Years)
1890	2.68	1902	7.94
1891	3.37	1903	6.57
1892	4.44	1904	7.75
1893	5.01	1905	7.81
1894	4.98	1906	9.49
1895	5.38	1907	8.62
1896	6.34	1908	9.02
1897	5.95	1909	9.72
1898	7.29	1910	9.74
1899	6.82	1911	10.9
1900	7.03	1912	10.3
1901	6.70		

[a] Measured at end of year.

thing would cease among the operators of cotton mills, the wage-earners would be better off. . . .[14]

Quite likely the extent of "raiding" in Alamance County was limited because so many of the local mills were controlled by the Holt family.

The average tenure of workers at the Alamance Mill tended to increase over time. The data presented in Table 2-1 indicate a secular upward trend in the average experience of the Alamance Mill workers. Table 2-2 details the remaining number of years that workers in 1890 and 1902, respectively, would continue to be employed by the Alamance Mill. The persistence

Table 2-2. Persistence of Alamance Mill Operatives:
Percentage of Workforce by Remaining Years of Service

| | Remaining Years of Service[a] | | | |
Year	1[b]	2–3	4–9	10+
1890	26[c]	14	31	30
1902	20	13	20	47

[a] Measured at beginning of year.

[b] One year or less; durations of less than a full year are recorded as a whole year.

[c] Includes irregular, part-time employees and full-time permanent operatives. Due to rounding, percentages do not always total to 100.

Table 2-3. Experience Composition of Alamance Mill Workforce: Percentage of Workforce with Given Number of Years of Cumulative Experience

Year	Number of Years of Experience[a]			
	1[b]	2–3	4–9	10+
1900	13	23	34	30
1910	8	19	32	41

[a] Cumulative experience measured at end of year.

[b] One year or less; 1 1/2 years experience is recorded as 2 years; similarly, 3 1/2 years is recorded as 4 years.

rates of the 1902 workforce tended to exceed the persistence rates for the 1890 workforce. For example, the proportion of the workforce who would still be employed 10 or more years later increased from 30 percent in 1890 to 47 percent in 1902. A comparison of the experience composition of the workforce in 1900 and 1910 in Table 2-3 further illustrates the secular trend. Another measure to be considered is the turnover of new workers. A worker initially entering the mill in 1891 tended to remain 2.25 years on average, but the average length of employment for a new recruit in 1905 was 3.7 years. Finally, the data for the 1902 workforce in Table 2-4 reveal the large degree of individual variation in duration of employment. Of the 18 operatives with one year or less experience in January 1902, 8 workers (44 percent) would leave within one year but 6 workers (33 percent) would stay at least 10 additional years. In contrast, of the 16 workers in 1902 who had already accrued at least 10 years' experience, all would remain a minimum of 4 more years, and 11 workers of this group would still be employed by the mill 10 years later.

Apparently the mills were generally successful in retaining a core group of stable workers along with the high-turnover workers. This stability was promoted by the family labor system and mill village paternalism. Nepotism and favoritism conferred advantages to long-term residents, increasing the cost of relocation for current mill village residents. Individual family members were not always free to relocate without jeopardizing the jobs of other family members. Mill owners exercised some degree of monopsony power within the mill village environs. Efforts to

Table 2-4. Duration of Employment, Alamance Mill Workforce, 1902: Persistence of Workers, by Years of Tenure

Individual blocks indicate number of workers with years of tenure given by row and remaining years of service by column.

Previous Years of Experience[a]	Persistence, Remaining Years of Service				Row Totals
	1	2–3	4–9	10+	
0–1	8	3	1	6	18(33%)
2–3	1	2	1	4	8(15%)
4–9	2	2	4	5	13(24%)
10+	–	–	5	11	16(29%)
Column totals	11 (20%)	7 (13%)	11 (20%)	26 (47%)	

[a]Measured at beginning of year.

increase the cost of quitting, such as family employment clauses or forfeiture of wages for inadequate notice upon quitting, diminished the frequency of voluntary departures further.

The problem of irregularity in attendance was acknowledged by August Kohn in 1903: "Every cotton mill in this state [South Carolina] recognizes that to have a full complement of labor in the mill each morning . . . it is practically necessary to carry a surplusage of 20 to 25 per cent of 'spare help.'"[15] High absenteeism tends to reduce productivity significantly. It was commonly assumed that permanent workers were simply unwilling to attend on a regular basis. However, as with aggregate turnover data, generalizations based upon average absentee rates may present a distorted or misleading characterization of the typical southern worker, because significant individual variation may exist. It is true that the payroll records of the Alamance Mill indicate many workers whose attendance was quite irregular or always part-time. These individuals worked fewer than 10 days out of a sample 8-week period during a given year. There were seven such workers in 1903 and 1905, four in 1904, and three or less for the rest of the years from 1890 to 1912. For exam-

Table 2-5. Percentage of Days Worked, Spinners and Weavers, by Region

	Spinners	Weavers	
North	61	56	(average of 10 firms)
South	49	43	(average of 5 firms)

Source: David P. Doane, "Regional Cost Differentials and Textile Location: A Statistical Analysis," *Explorations in Economic History* 9 (Fall 1971): 21.

ple, one female employee worked only four days in a two-month period in 1894, none in 1895, four in 1886, one in 1897, none in 1898, and was absent one-half of the days in 1899. Nevertheless, the group of casual workers never comprised more than 8 percent of the workforce.

In a study comparing attendance records for the textile industry in 1890, David Doane concluded that "northern workers [were] more reliable than their southern counterparts."[16] His data are presented in Table 2-5. In addition, Doane suggested that these data support the claim by Melvin Copeland in 1912 that southern workers were "fickle" or lax in their attendance. As Doane surveyed an atypical sample of mills, his conclusions may not necessarily be applicable to the majority of southern cotton mills. He selected a group of mills in which weavers were paid on a daily flat-rate basis. However, in most southern mills, weavers were remunerated on a piece-rate basis, as in the Alamance Mill. Further, Doane suggested that, in general, spinners tended to have more regular attendance than weavers; however, for the Alamance Mill in 1895, the absentee rate for weavers was less than 1 percent.

Furthermore, the number of days worked is not solely under the control of the individual worker. During 1879 it was reported in a diary of a manager of the Alamance Mill that heavy rains forced the temporary closure of the mill. "Rain began falling Sunday 2 ocl AM & by 2PM the water was 6 inc in the weave room." Before steam power was introduced, low water levels also halted production. Nonetheless, during 1879 workers staged a "slowdown" in protest of work assignment on the day after Easter, a day that was traditionally considered a work holiday. "Factory runing on Ester Monday such never was the case before [*sic*], hands all mad & not much good done that day."[17] For the year 1895, the Alamance Mill payroll records indicate 29 days when a significant majority of all workers did not work, excluding Sundays. On such days, it is quite probable that it was an administrative decision to discontinue operations temporarily, not a mere whim of unruly workers refusing to perform their jobs. During the same year, the rate of "voluntary" absenteeism among workers (excluding irregular, part-time workers) was 4 percent of the total workdays per month.

Mill wage rates significantly affected the supply of labor that could be mobilized. As the wage represented an essential aspect of the job package offered to attract workers, the remainder of this chapter investigates the major determinants of individual earnings at the Alamance Mill.

To analyze the dispersion of individual wages at the Alamance Mill, earnings functions were estimated for each year from 1890 to 1912. (The source materials and the preparation of the data are described in Appendix A.) An earnings or wage function relates the wages offered by the mill to characteristics or traits of the individual workers. A generally accepted semi-log formulation for the earnings function is used:[18]

$$\log \text{earnings} = \alpha_0 + \beta_i X_i \qquad i = 1, \ldots, n \qquad (1)$$

The set of independent variables considered here, the X_i, includes experience, experience squared, age, and dummy variables for sex and literacy. Earnings data were derived from the daily payroll records. The dependent variable is the logarithm of the full-time weekly earnings. The experience variable is the tenure or number of years of employment at the Alamance Mill. Age and the ability of a worker to read and write were determined by matching names on the payroll with the Manuscript Census schedules for the years 1900 and 1910. In a given year the mill employed between 50 and 70 workers, and during the 23-year period, 271 individuals were employed full time for varying lengths of time. The cross-section regression results are reported in Tables 2-6 and 2-7. The estimation yields the result that experience and sex were important determinants of wages but that age and education were not.

The regression results reported in Table 2-6 generally support the conclusion that experience or length of employment in the Alamance Mill had a significant positive influence on individual earnings.[19] Management strongly believed that skills

Table 2-6. Estimated Earnings Functions, Alamance Mill, Entire Workforce

Log earnings $= \alpha_0 + \beta_1$ experience $+ \beta_2$ (experience)$^2 + \beta_3$ sex

Year	Constant	Experience	(Experience)^2	Sex	r^2
1890	1.29	0.79	−.002	−.204	.25
	(8.37)	(.972)	(−.323)	(−2.60)	
1891	1.13	.173	−.009	−.187	.32
	(6.38)	(2.52)	(−1.80)	(−2.32)	
1892	1.00	.151	−.007	−.142	.29
	(4.41)	(2.26)	(−1.52)	(−1.53)	
1893	1.02	.089	−.002	−.087	.27
	(5.45)	(1.64)	(−.58)	(−1.02)	
1894	1.19	.038	.000	−.119	.26
	(9.68)	(1.15)		(−1.64)	
1895	1.08	.084	−.002	−.191	.28
	(6.77)	(2.35)	(−1.04)	(−2.05)	
1896	.653	.117	−.003	.000	.37
	(3.50)	(3.08)	(−1.62)		
1897	.765	.127	−.004	−.066	.37
	(4.90)	(3.78)	(−2.27)	(−.774)	
1898	.856	.152	−.005	−.210	.46
	(4.77)	(4.12)	(−2.77)	(−2.33)	
1899	1.03	.091	−.003	−.153	.30
	(5.65)	(2.64)	(−1.67)	(−1.69)	
1900	.854	.124	−.004	−.081	.32
	(4.95)	(3.92)	(−2.98)	(−.892)	
1901	1.07	.086	−.003	−.114	.34
	(8.01)	(3.44)	(−2.32)	(−1.44)	
1902	1.05	.070	−.002	−.080	.30
	(7.91)	(2.80)	(−1.82)	(−1.01)	
1903	1.09	.073	−.002	−.059	.25
	(10.2)	(3.29)	(−2.20)	(−.812)	
1904	1.20	.045	−.001	−.038	.20
	(12.3)	(2.44)	(−1.54)	(−.678)	
1905	1.24	.052	−.001	−.080	.36
	(17.2)	(3.83)	(−2.54)	(−1.85)	
1906	1.33	.050	−.001	−.117	.37
	(16.6)	(3.67)	(−2.53)	(−2.66)	
1907	1.47	.045	−.0009	−.141	.41
	(14.3)	(2.72)	(−1.57)	(−2.94)	
1908	1.65	.020	−.0002	−.152	.33
	(15.1)	(1.27)	(−.292)	(−3.17)	
1909	1.84	.012	.0000	−.226	.37
	(17.7)	(.817)		(−4.82)	
1910	1.56	.036	−.0007	−.211	.36
	(14.9)	(2.36)	(−1.46)	(−2.76)	

Table 2-6 (continued)

Year	Constant	Experience	$(\text{Experience})^2$	Sex	r^2
1911	1.63	.041	−.0008	−.169	.36
	(14.1)	(2.84)	(−1.84)	(−3.25)	
1912	1.61	.036	−.0006	−.171	.32
	(16.2)	(2.64)	(−1.53)	(−3.28)	

Note: *t*-statistics in parentheses.

required to produce high-quality cloth were acquired through experience and on-the-job training. A mill manager in Cleveland County stated in 1891, "We advance every year in our capacity to make a better class of goods. Labor is becoming better trained, and wages increase in proportion."[20] An experienced, trained worker would require less supervision and guidance in the production process. When the skilled veteran cloth dyer at the Odell Manufacturing Company became ill in 1888, the manager wrote in a personal letter: "Our dyer here is very sick, and I have put an entirely 'green' hand in the Dye House to learn the business, but of course I have to spend a great deal of my time in there."[21] Nonetheless, it was expected that the novice worker would gradually acquire the requisite knowledge and skills to work independently.

More experienced workers thus received higher pay because on-the-job training increased their proficiency, resulting in real gains in productivity.[22] Furthermore, the model developed by Joanne Salop and Steven Salop suggests that a portion of the experience wage differential may have represented a payment for stability to minimize turnover or hiring costs.[23] Although newly hired workers were remunerated at relatively low lev-

Table 2-7. Estimated Earnings Functions, Alamance Mill Workers

Log earnings $= \alpha_0 + \beta_1\text{age} + \beta_2\text{sex} + \beta_3\text{experience} + \beta_4\text{literacy}$

Year	Constant	Age	Sex	Experience	Literacy	n	r^2
1900	1.12	.005	−.016	.021	−.238	42	.36
	(4.83)	(.614)	(−.126)	(1.77)	(−1.70)		
1910	1.63	.007	−.199	.077	−.026	49	.39
	(12.6)	(1.19)	(−2.22)	(.976)	(−.282)		

Note: *t*-statistics in parentheses.

Table 2-8. Estimated Earnings Functions, Alamance Mill, the Weavers

Log earnings $= \alpha_0 + \beta_1$ experience $+ \beta_2$ (experience)$^2 + \beta_3$ sex

Year	Constant	Experience	(Experience)^2	Sex	r^2
1890	1.49	−.020	.003	−.210	.42
	(13.8)	(−4.68)	(.861)	(−2.59)	
1891	1.53	−.005	−.001	−.147	.27
	(13.3)	(−.112)	(.327)	(−2.08)	
1892	1.44	.001	−.0004	−.112	.28
	(12.2)	(.016)	(.174)	(−1.50)	
1893	1.47	.040	−.002	−.192	.51
	(16.4)	(1.58)	(−1.21)	(−2.74)	
1894	1.41	.023	−.001	−.125	.20
	(13.9)	(.734)	(−.492)	(−1.50)	
1895	1.41	.047	−.003	−.258	.43
	(15.0)	(1.80)	(−1.74)	(−3.13)	
1896	1.42	.064	−.004	−2.62	.46
	(7.71)	(1.92)	(−1.98)	(−2.19)	
1897	1.27	.091	−.005	−.174	.51
	(6.65)	(2.60)	(−.024)	(−1.57)	
1898	1.47	.051	−.002	−.163	.46
	(8.58)	(1.70)	(−1.75)	(−1.89)	
1899	1.65	.015	−.001	−.203	.42
	(16.1)	(.967)	(−1.51)	(−2.64)	
1900	1.78	.011	−.001	−.279	.73
	(12.4)	(.467)	(−1.40)	(−4.29)	
1901	1.45	.044	−.002	−.158	.43
	(12.2)	(1.93)	(−1.77)	(−1.61)	

els, individual workers could expect regular advances as they accrued experience with the firm. Also, differential rewards were made available to long-term residents of mill villages through the practice of nepotism and favoritism. The favoritism may have been reflected in systematic variation in job assignments or the most desirable company-subsidized housing may have been allocated to the long-term residents. Low initial wages with increases based on tenure would be less attractive to a potential job applicant with a high propensity to quit than would smooth or level earnings. Hence, through a self-selection process, the high-turnover worker was less likely to apply for employment while the low-turnover worker was still attracted by the promise of predictable wage advances. The tiered-system of earnings based on experience would, in effect, shift the costs of

Table 2-8 *(continued)*

Year	Constant	Experience	(Experience)^2	Sex	r^2
1902	1.48 (16.6)	.032 (1.59)	−.001 (−1.46)	−.163 (−1.92)	.36
1903	1.47 (11.8)	.002 (.066)	−.000	.060 (.461)	.03
1904	1.49 (31.0)	.022 (2.11)	−.0001 (−2.05)	−.183 (−3.87)	.57
1905	1.45 (16.8)	.036 (2.15)	−.001 (−1.91)	−.178 (−2.40)	.52
1906	1.35 (11.6)	.054 (2.47)	−.002 (−2.27)	−.170 (−2.02)	.51
1907	1.70 (9.90)	.006 (.180)	−.0001 (.0873)	−.305 (−2.43)	.54
1908	1.74 (8.77)	.017 (.523)	−.0003 (−.273)	−.253 (−1.81)	.37
1909	1.71 (7.77)	.038 (1.11)	−.001 (−.886)	−.241 (−1.98)	.48
1910	1.83 (6.34)	.038 (.904)	−.001 (−.403)	−.082 (−.611)	.19
1911	1.65 (8.75)	.040 (1.35)	−.001 (−1.17)	−.080 (−.539)	.25
1912	1.64 (6.10)	.021 (.607)	−.001 (−.403)	−.040 (−.271)	.10

Note: *t*-statistics in parentheses.

high turnover to the employee in the form of foregone wages during the first years of employment.[24] Therefore, the wage differential for experience was justified on the basis of both current productivity differences as well as the desire to minimize total turnover costs by offering a payment for stability.[25]

The earnings of the weavers represent an apparent exception to the pattern that more experienced workers tended to receive higher pay. The weavers were identifiable as a distinct group of workers in one occupation who were paid on a uniform piece-rate basis.[26] The coefficients on experience for the weaver group presented in Table 2-8 generally are not significantly different from zero. This puzzling result may be explained by the existence of a minimum level of experience required to qualify to become a weaver. Young workers frequently entered the mill as doffers or spinners. Only after they acquired skill and experience were some workers then transferred to the weaving room. Weavers tended to earn more on average than most

workers. Experience likely was a major prerequisite for entry
into this lucrative occupation, but once the promotion was
attained, additional experience exerted much less upward pressure on earnings. Hence the importance of experience as an
influence upon the earnings of this set of workers would be
hidden from the data.

The regression results in Table 2-6 provide evidence of a
declining contribution of experience to earnings over time. The
values of the estimated coefficients on experience in Table 2-6
tended to shift to a lower level after the turn of the century.
This pattern may reflect the diminishing returns to additional
years of experience over time as the industry matured. The
structure of the wage contract was gradually altered as the pool
of experienced workers grew. Given the growth of the cotton
textile industry during the postbellum period, the pool of experienced workers expanded independently of any change in individual persistence rates.[27] The incentive structure of the wage
contract tended to attract families who would stay with one mill
for a long period of time. Even with no change in individual
quit propensities, a large core group of "stayers" or workers
with low quit propensities would gradually accumulate. As mill
owners found it easier to secure an experienced workforce,
the premium payment for stability was eliminated. Mill managers would have tolerated an increase in the turnover rate over
time if the recruitment and training costs for securing a compe-
tent worker declined as the supply of experienced workers expanded.

Supplementing the selective recruitment efforts, mill managers also developed strategies designed to lower the quit
propensities of the workers actually hired. The stabilizing
influences of the family labor system and the comprehensive
welfare program increased the strength of the attachment of
the family to the mill, thereby diminishing quit propensities.
Since the Holt family owned most of the surrounding mills in
the county, possibilities for mobility were particularly limited.
The mill village tended to draw the families together in a shared
bond of community identity. With all major social and economic
activity centered in the mill village, mill paternalism tended to
bind the family to the mill setting. Given the emergence of an
expanding group of workers permanently attached to the mill, a
smaller fraction of the productivity gains from additional expe-

rience was passed on to the worker and the payment for stability was reduced. Hence, the contribution of experience to earnings declined over time.

Relative wages in the Alamance Mill were significantly influenced by the sex of the operatives as well as by the accumulated level of experience.[28] In the regression equations in Tables 2-6 and 2-7, the sex of the workers was entered as a dummy variable (sex = 0 if male, 1 if female), such that a negative coefficient on sex indicates that females tended to receive lower earnings than males. Females tended to earn significantly less than males in about half of the years of study when we control for the influence of experience.[29] The relatively weak influence of sex as a determinant of earnings for many years is somewhat surprising. This may be the consequence of the emphasis upon the family unit rather than the individual, male or female, in the job bargaining process. Also, the primary, head-of-household wage-earner was often a female.

In assessing the contribution of sex as a determinant of wages, the above procedure of dummy variables effectively constrained the slope of the regression lines but allowed for different estimated intercepts for the male and female earnings functions. An alternative method can also be employed which allows the slope to vary between the two groups of workers, males and females. The basic model for this purpose is expressed in equation 2:

$$\ln(Y) = \alpha_0 + \beta_1 \exp \qquad (2)$$

where $\ln(Y)$ = natural log of earnings

$\exp$ = experience

Separate equations are estimated for each group of workers. The estimated equations for 1891 are presented as equations 3 and 4:

$$\ln(Y)_{\text{male}} = \alpha_m + \beta_m \exp \qquad m = \text{male}$$
$$\ln(Y)_{\text{male}} = 1.04 + .065 \exp \qquad (3)$$
$$(8.64) \ (3.50)$$

$$\ln(Y)_{\text{female}} = \alpha_f + \beta_f \exp \qquad f = \text{female}$$
$$\ln(Y)_{\text{female}} = 1.00 + .035 \exp \qquad (4)$$
$$(12.0) \ (1.66)$$

(t-statistics are in parentheses)

The estimated difference between the two groups is found to be significant by analysis of covariance, confirming the conclusion that sex was an important determinant of earnings. Similar findings are obtained for five years of the study.

The larger estimated value of the coefficient of experience for males than for females in equations 3 and 4 may be partially explained by the greater range of opportunities or occupations open to males. The lowest paying occupation in the mill, doffing, was traditionally reserved for young boys at the entry level. At the other extreme, the most skilled and managerial positions commanding the highest wages were limited to experienced males. Females were excluded from the occupations of superintendent, loom fixer, and foreman.

The extent of sexual discrimination reflected in the male-female wage differential may be estimated by a technique developed by Alan Blinder.[30] Blinder has suggested a procedure for decomposing the male-female wage differential into two components: the portion attributable to differences in objective traits such as experience and the portion deriving from discrimination.

Again with reference to equations 3 and 4 for 1891, the unexplained portion of the differential captured by the constant coefficients is $\alpha_m - \alpha_f = .04$. The explained portion of the differential $(\beta_m \overline{X}_m) - (\beta_f \overline{X}_f)$ may be rewritten in the form

$$\beta_m(\overline{X}_m - \overline{X}_f) + \overline{X}_f(\beta_m - \beta_f) = 0.078 + .076 \qquad (5)$$
where $\overline{X}$ = average experience.

The final term of the above expression yields a 7.6 percent wage differential in favor of males "which exists only because the market evaluates differently the identical bundle of traits if possessed by members of different demographic groups [and this] is a reflection of discrimination as much as the shift coefficient is."[31] With Blinder's technique of decomposition, a 7.8 percent wage advantage in favor of males (from equation 5) is attributable to the greater average experience of males. More importantly, the sum of the differential captured by the constant coefficient and the final term of equation 5 yields an 11.6 percent wage differential attributable to discrimination.[32]

The gradient of the earnings function is steeper for males (equation 3) than for females (equation 4). The policy of

advancing men to the better jobs perhaps should be understood in conjunction with the apparent policy of offering a rising earnings gradient in order to induce self-selection of the
more persistent workers. If the delayed reward, or wage premium for stability, were differentially made available to males
and females and other factors remained equal, we would expect
higher turnover rates for females than males. In 1900, the average experience for males was 8.2 years and the average experience for females was 7.0 years, possibly suggesting greater
turnover among females.[33] Perhaps a portion of the calculated
7.8 percent wage advantage attributable to an "objective trait,"
the greater average experience of males, may also reflect sexual
discrimination.

Nevertheless, although the existence of sex discrimination has
been detected, real productivity differences also account for
a portion of the male-female wage differential. As the group
of weavers was compensated on a uniform piece-rate basis,
higher wages imply greater output per worker. When the log-
arithms of earnings of the weavers are regressed on experience, experience squared, and the sex dummy for each of the
23 years, as Table 2-8 shows, the expected significant negative
sign on the sex coefficient is obtained for several years. The
estimated coefficient on the dummy variable for sex for a year
such as 1900 suggests that real productivity differences existed
between the sexes, perhaps relating to the greater strength and
endurance of males. Therefore, sex wage differentials were not
merely the result of discrimination or screening mechanisms
that filtered males into higher paying occupations. Alternatively,
women perhaps did not have incentive to try as hard or work
as intensively as males because of the limited opportunities for
advancement open to them.

In addition to experience and sex, the age of the worker was
also considered as a determinant of individual earnings. The
age data were drawn from the 1900 and 1910 Manuscript Census schedules. The estimated values for the coefficient on age in
Table 2-7 are not significantly different from zero. Age would
be positively correlated with experience. With multicollinear-
ity, the precision of estimation declines, preventing an accu-
rate assessment of the influence of age and maturity. Given the
incentive structure of the family labor system, the mill attracted

both mature adults and their older children as workers. Chapter 3 presents the rationale for the employment of workers of various ages and maturity.

The final independent variable considered in the estimation of the earnings function is worker literacy. When the dummy variable for literacy is included in the regression models in Table 2-7, the estimated coefficients on education are not significantly different from zero. This result is startling, given the substantial commitment of resources to schooling by southern cotton textile mills. However, this does not exclude the possibility that education of the mill village children made some significant contribution to production that was captured by the companies. Experience, education, and skill of the workforce were thought to be crucial determinants of the quality of output. Although the mill managers recognized the benefits to be derived from an educated workforce, perhaps the direct productivity increase due to the education of an individual worker was too difficult to ascertain to influence relative earnings or literacy may not be a sufficiently sensitive indicator of educational variation. Mill records show that several of the illiterate workers were weavers, a relatively high-paying occupation. For the weaving function, perhaps on-the-job training provided a substitute for education, or actual experience may have been more valuable to skill acquisition than formal education. As no strong conclusions regarding the impact of education can be drawn from the regression results, an assessment of the role of schooling within the context of the family labor system is provided in Chapter 4.[34]

The cotton mill villages provided the foundations or centers for the major social and economic activities of the cotton mill operatives and their families. The control of workers by management, however, is never absolute. Despite the strength and pervasiveness of mill paternalism, the workers retained an identity independent of the cotton mill. The findings presented in this chapter have suggested that the structure of earnings and working conditions reflected the challenges confronting mill management in recruiting and training a corps of factory operatives.

3

The Employment
of Family Workers

The adoption of the family labor system led mill managers to
employ workers of varied ages, including children. The conditions of child labor were discussed as a social issue by humanitar-
ians, educators, public officials, union sympathizers, and even
some mill managers. Progressive reformers, such as Felix Adler,
actively advocated the abolition of child labor: "The emancipation of childhood from economic servitude is a social reform of
the first magnitude."[1] Very strong sentiments of moral indigna-
tion and outrage were expressed by Edwin Markham in 1906:

> In the Southern cotton mills . . . we find a gaunt goblin army of
> children keeping their forced march on the factory-floors—an army
> that outwatches the sun by day and the stars by night . . . —a spectral
> army of pigmy people sucked in from the hills to dance beside the
> crazing wheels.[2]

Alternatively, the more moderate position taken by Holland
Thompson emphasized that child labor merely reflected the
relative underdevelopment and low income levels of the South:

> The employers are not primarily to blame for the evils of child labor.
> Such labor is simply a stage in the development of an industrial
> society. The great number of families coming from the farms are the

raw material out of which a skilled labor force is to be developed.
Necessarily there are difficulties in adjustment.

The phenomenon is always present in an industrial transition.
Hours were longer and conditions harder in England, in the *same
stage* of industrial development.[3]

This chapter examines the employment of children as an
economic, rather than as a moral or social, phenomenon. It
addresses certain questions about the integral role of child labor
within the family labor system, such as: How did the employment of children influence family welfare? Was the class of
child workers treated as a distinct group within a dual or segmented labor market? And, why did mills continue to employ
young operatives even though managers apparently regarded
them as the most costly and troublesome workers?

The composition of the cotton textile workforce in the South
was provided in Table 1-1. During 1909, 18.9 percent of the
wage earners in the cotton goods industry in North Carolina
were children under 16, contrasting with only 5.7 percent of
the workforce in Massachusetts.[4]

The earnings of children employed in the mills contributed
to the welfare of their families. The level of total family income
was likely of greater importance in the decision to migrate to the
mill village than the wages of any one individual family member.
Generally the potential earnings of the head-of-household alone
were considered inadequate to support a family in the mill
village. Therefore, individual parents felt compelled to supplement their meager earnings by allowing their children to work
in the mill. Although a higher family income would tend to
improve family material welfare, there may have been other off-
setting negative dimensions of child labor which are discussed
later in this chapter. The move to the mill signified an improvement in the standard of living. As one worker commented in
1891, "I think we can do better here than we can on a farm."[5]

Furthermore, from a life-cycle perspective, a child's increase
in productivity resulting from experience gained on the job
would translate into higher mill earnings in successive years.
The econometric results presented in Chapter 2 indicate that
experience was positively associated with earnings. Resources
invested in on-the-job training improved worker productivity.
Child labor was important in developing a skilled, well-socialized
workforce. Although children were not themselves considered

superior operatives by mill managers, it was widely believed that the best time to begin the training and development of the workforce was at a young age. It was taken for granted that more mature workers provided the most satisfactory labor services and that it was imperative to initiate the children into the work setting at a young age to achieve ultimately the best workforce. To a great extent, schooling and work experience were considered substitutes in the acquisition of the skills necessary to earn a living as an adult. According to one mill manager: "Industry is an education."[6] The mature worker who had initially entered the mill as a child was considered by management to be the more valuable worker. As one mill manager observed:

> from the ages of ten to fourteen years children can be taught more readily and more thoroughly to do efficient cotton mill work than at any other age, and because, as a majority of these children will have to depend on the labor of their hands for their livelihood, they should learn thoroughly to do efficient work as a part of their education.[7]

However, the Department of Labor stated in 1904 that the unrestricted power of the parents to force their children to work diminished the incentives of older family members to work diligently. The labor of children could thus be perceived as "surplus labor" in the sense that family income could be maintained without the employment of the younger members if the remaining workers were willing to work harder.[8] Perhaps total family productivity would not decline if only the older members applied themselves with increased vigor. "In many instances had the older members of the family worked with greater energy the labor of many young children, at least of those under 12, might have been spared without any diminution in the family income."[9]

Moreover, it has been argued that the supply of child workers tended to depress the general level of wages received by adults. Claudia Goldin and Donald Parsons have estimated that for the United States in 1890, for each $1.00 annual increment in child workers' earnings, the earnings of the male head-of-household were reduced by $.71.[10] If all parents collectively withdrew their children from the labor force, the resulting rise in wages would have lessened the pressure to send children into the mills. One might argue that the elimination of children from labor force participation would contract the total labor supply, reducing the quantity of labor offered at each real wage level. In order for businesses to attract sufficient labor, the new labor market equilibrium would dictate a rise in wages and a redistribution of income toward adult workers.

The above argument, which predicts that adult wages would have been higher in the absence of child labor, fails to recognize that the labor force participation of several family members was central to the internal logic of the system of labor organization that emerged in the industry. The character and complexion of the workforce and the population in the mill village would have been dramatically altered had children been barred from employment in the early stages of the postbellum industrial expansion. It is less likely that the mills would have initially induced whole families to migrate from the farm to the company town without the possibility for gainful employment for the young family members. Hence it is improbable that a rise in the adult wage sufficient to compensate for the direct loss in earnings of the children under 16 would have been realized by the family units who actually moved to the mill village.[11] The family unit was the relevant unit of labor in labor negotiations. The organization of labor based on the family unit was management's response to the need to secure a factory workforce. As previously discussed, the family labor system played a vital role in the dual personnel functions of initial recruitment and the continuing development of a stable, disciplined workforce. Recruitment costs were minimized by attracting mature workers who brought with them additional workers. The costs of housing, extension of credit for moving expenses, and other welfare activities provided to the family were spread over several workers. Also, child labor was viewed as an investment or strategy for securing an experienced adult workforce.

Apart from the value of the foregone earnings, an increase in leisure associated with the withdrawal of a youth from mill work did not necessarily represent an unambiguous improvement in family welfare. Microeconomic theory conceives of leisure time as an economic good that an individual considers when deciding how best to use his time. However, if greater weight is attached to the preferences of parents in deciding how the family uses its time, the increase in leisure time for children may not necessarily be perceived as an improvement in family welfare. It was thought that if boys were excluded from the mill, they would be tempted to run wild in the streets, acquire bad habits, and be exposed to immoral influences. There were strong mores against idleness and vagrancy, reflecting the paternalistic attitude of management discussed in Chapter 2. A mill manager claimed that village children who were not attending school or working in the mill tended to "loaf around on the back alleys more than half of their time and learn more villainy [*sic*]."[12] Stronger sentiments were expressed by a mill secretary-treasurer: "I think the worst thing you can do for a boy is to let him be idle. I had rather mine were working, even if they did not earn anything."[13] Of course, the above remark conveys the overtone of moral guidance by management that pervaded the mill village.

The state of an individual's health serves as one indicator of socioeconomic well being.[14] Therefore, the exposure of children to a hazardous or unhealthful environment in the factory would negatively influence the child's welfare. Certainly the working day was quite long for the young operatives. The mills were often hot, humid, and noisy. The prolonged exposure to lint and dust in the air is associated with the progressive development of byssinosis, a respiratory ailment. However, children were generally excluded from occupations (such as picking and carding) with the greatest exposure to dust-laden air. Although the frequency of accidents among youth was relatively high, the occupations with the highest probability of severe injury were filled by adult workers only. In a study of 523 on-the-job accidents in 89 southern mills in 1906, 25.2 percent of the cases involved workers 15 years of age or younger.[15]

The observation that many mill children were found to be in poor health does not necessarily imply that the factory environment was the culprit. The workforce was composed of a large proportion of destitute farmers who had only recently migrated to the industrial sector. The poorest farm families undoubtedly suffered severe deficiencies in nutrition and sanitation, and these were the families who were likely to move to the mill village. Therefore, many of the health problems were actually rooted in the farm sector and transplanted to the mill village. A Senate report concluded that "the so-called 'cotton mill anemia' and the stunted development of many of the cotton mill minors of the Gulf-Atlantic States are the direct result of hookworm

infection rather than of mill work."[16] The report estimated that
the transfer of 100 new mill operatives from the farm introduced 29 cases of hookworm disease to the mill village.[17] Despite
the improvement in sanitation in the mill village, eradication of
the disease was slowed by its persistence for up to twelve years.

The Senate report also found that the sanitary conditions
were generally superior in the mill villages than on the farms.
As a result, the incidence of suspected cases of hookworm disease was lower in the mill villages populated by many second-
generation mill workers than in the mills where most workers
had only recently transferred from the farms. To support this
conclusion, the health of workers at two mills, located 1 1/2 miles
apart and operated under the same management, was investigated by a team of health officials. The mills afforded comparable sanitary conditions, but in one mill, many of the workers
had been born and raised in the mill village; in the second case,
most workers had only recently transferred from the farm. The
findings of the study are reported in Table 3-1.

In contrast, in his study of the New England cotton textile
industry of 1900, Mark Aldrich stated that "Millwork seems to
have been a cause of general excess mortality."[18] He demon-
strated that the self-selectivity bias imposed by the initial hiring of many unhealthy individuals was relatively weak. Aldrich
also found that age-adjusted death rates tended to increase with
long experience, a result inconsistent with a strong "sickly worker" effect. He therefore concluded that millwork was a risky,
hazardous occupation. The observation of differential rates in
childhood mortality by the parent's occupation further tends to
confirm the riskiness of the occupation. For native white women
within the textile industry in the United States for the year 1900,
the ratio of actual child deaths to the expected number of child
deaths per 1000 women was 1.20, indicating that child mortality
among this group of women was high relative to the national
average.[19]

Furthermore, confinement in the factory at an early age
may have been deleterious to the well-being of a child because
opportunities for recreation and creative play were limited.
Monotonous, mindless work is generally considered a grave
social problem, and the damaging consequences for youthful
workers would be seriously compounded. If the work environment does not provide a source of stimulation and the child

Table 3-1. The Incidence of Suspected Cases of Hookworm Disease in the First and Second Generation of Mill Life

	Proportion of Workers with Hookworm Disease	
	All Ages Combined (%)	Under 16 Years (%)
First generation mill	21.6	43.7
Second generation mill	3.5	5.7
Difference	18.1	38.0

Source: U.S. Commissioner of Labor, *Report on Condition of Woman and Child Wage-Earners in the United States*, Senate Document #645, 61st Cong., 2d sess., vol. 17, *Hookworm Disease among Cotton-Mill Operatives* (Washington, D.C.: Government Printing Office, 1912): 34.

is exposed to this environment for 10 to 12 hours per day, the blossoming of the power of creative expression is stifled. Aesthetic needs would go unfulfilled. Opponents of child labor argued that the child operative passively responded to factory directives without actively seeking to change or comprehend the environment of the work process. Edgar Murphy, a philanthropist opposed to child labor, opined: "In the factory, the child is just a child, an anonymous, practically unknown member of a pathetic industrial aggregate known as 'the child workers.'"[20] In contrast, a mill advocate declared that children on the mountain farms never played because they simply did not know how; therefore, the stimulation and discipline of the mill and village environment represented a positive influence on the development of a youth.[21]

The employment of children in the mill was not generally perceived as unjust exploitation of the labor services of youth. Migration to the mill village did not signal the initiation of the children into servitude or even their introduction to gainful employment. From a young age, children had been expected to supplement the labor of their parents on the farm. Although these children were not always officially recorded as farm laborers for the official census reports, their labor contribution was not insignificant, particularly at harvest time. During the period of peak seasonal labor demand, the length of the child's working day on the farm was greater than that of the mill. Moreover, the physical strain of manual farm labor exceeded the level of exertion demanded in the mill.

One interesting question that arises is whether children and adults competed for the same jobs in the labor market. The most skilled and lucrative occupations such as foreman and superintendent were open only to adult males. The more objectionable type of work would fall upon the children if they were considered the casual workers. An employee in a mill in Richmond County, North Carolina, complained in 1887 that "the employment of children in the mills at low wages keeps a great many men out of employment."[22] Did the existence of the family system of labor lessen the stratification of the labor market into two segmented, noncompeting groups?

Labor market segmentation is perceived by Michael Reich, David Gordon, and Richard Edwards to be the historical response to political and economic forces deriving from the emergence of monopoly capital.[23] The segmentation of the workforce facilitated the filtering of workers into factory occupations that were gradually becoming more stratified. Separate "entry ports" and job ladders served to "fit" workers into the emerging capitalist class structure. The segmentation gave legitimacy to the increasing inequality among workers, reinforcing the industrial authority of managers. The labor market became fragmented into two submarkets, the primary and secondary workforces. The main determinants for inclusion within each category relate to group characteristics, rather than individual traits. In the primary sector, wages tend to be relatively high, advancement possibilities exist, and moderate job security or work regularity prevails. In contrast, the secondary market is distinguished by lower wages, greater workload instability, and the absence of substantive job ladders. The jobs relegated to the secondary workers typically do not demand steady work habits. The attributes of the secondary class of workers should be examined with reference to the group of child workers to determine if the labor was effectively stratified into distinct classes.

To examine this segmentation, it is necessary to discuss the decision to relocate from the farm to the mill. This decision was made by the parents based upon expected improvement in the standard of living. Subsequently, as a condition of mill employment, the children were often required to work as well. Although a premium over farm earnings was offered, wages remained low enough in absolute terms to force the family to accept the obligation of labor services performed by the children. Thus,

Table 3-2. Hourly Earnings of Employees in All Occupations, North Carolina Cotton Mills, 1907

Age	Number		Earnings per Hour	
	Male	Female	Male	Female
<11 years	42	23	.044	.047
11 years	57	36	.052	.056
12 years	170	159	.055	.058
13 years	261	210	.060	.065
14 years	340	299	.067	.070
15 years	273	311	.072	.087
16 years	169	338	.032	.082
17 years	98	300	.099	.089
18 years	141	391	.105	.091
19 years	95	266	.119	.090
20 years	140	265	.120	.093
21 years	120	190	.119	.097
22 years	111	159	.124	.096
23 years	72	111	.134	.097
24 years	89	80	.131	.102
25 to 29	282	322	.137	.101
30 to 34	165	158	.133	.106
35 to 39	71	76	.135	.096

Source: U.S. Commissioner of Labor, *Report on Condition of Woman and Child Wage-Earners in the United States,* Senate Document #645, 61st Cong., 2d sess., vol. 1 (Washington, D.C.: Government Printing Office, 1910): 314.

the children were a "captive workforce," identifiable as a group by their age and subject to unequal ranking.

The filtering of children into jobs demanding the least individual initiative and responsibility tended to preserve traditional social hierarchical relations. The older members of the family were often expected to supervise and control the younger members in the mill, preserving traditional roles of authority within the family. The mill management was comprised entirely of adult males, affirming the patriarchal dominance of the society.

Young workers earned less on average than adult workers. For 1890 Harry Douty estimated that average annual earnings for men, women, and children in North Carolina were $254, $159, and $90, respectively.[24] The data on earnings by age presented in Table 3-2 exhibit a distinct upward trend. Although it has been stated frequently that children were paid at the same

rate as adults when they performed identical tasks,[25] perhaps
this only means that the piece rate was uniform, allowing for
systematic variation in the job assignment.

With regard to the stability of the work, children were frequently considered the casual workers to be drawn into the mill
as needed to cope with the variability of workload requirements.
The village schools, financially supported by the mills, were sub-
ordinated to the daily and seasonal fluctuating labor demands of
the mills. Commenting on the Alamance school, one mill worker
recalled that "they ran it in the summers when the mill could
not run on account of low water."[26]

The occupation of doffing itself contributed to the socialization of workers and the inculcation of traits of stability and
steady work habits. An intense, rapid pace of work for perhaps
40 minutes alternated with 20 minutes of free time or recess.
During the respite from the work regimentation, the boys were
allowed to go outside and play or just sit by the windowsill
and "while away the time" for the remainder of the hour. The
recurring pattern of work followed by controlled play gradually conditioned the child to adapt to the routine of mechan-
ical production. In 1907 the median age for doffers was 14
and more than 98 percent of all doffers were younger than 21,
suggesting that doffing was an occupation intended exclusively
for children.[27] For this occupation, children and adults were
essentially noncompeting groups. The job itself did not require
sober attentive work habits, but gradually the worker's attention
span would be lengthened and his rambunctious nature quieted
sufficiently to transfer the worker to another activity.

Although age represented a group characteristic upon which
stratification was predicated, the mobility between the groups
within the mill was effected with the passage of time. Thus,
strict labor market segmentation did not prevail. Child workers continued to work and advance in the mill as they reached
adulthood. This is in marked contrast to the parish apprentice-
ship system in England where the majority of the young male
textile workers no longer were able to obtain jobs in the mills
when they reached adulthood.[28]

That entry ports into the primary positions were eventually
opened to the child operatives was therefore not the direct consequence of the nature of textile production per se but rather

was a characteristic of the form of labor organization adopted in the southern cotton textile industry. The comprehensive welfare system of the southern mill village was designed to stabilize the labor force and produce a class of hereditary mill workers. The paternalistic system can be viewed as a deliberate strategy to ensure that the child workers would remain in the employ of the mill. The child was pressured by the system to make the transition from child worker to adult worker within the cotton textile establishment.

Perhaps a case could be presented that segmentation was predicated upon sex and not age.[29] The workforce was divided into three groups: adult males, adult females, and children. Although the average earnings of young girls often exceeded those of young boys, the potential advancement for boys far exceeded that available for girls. (Refer to Table 3-2.) Both girls and boys would eventually be transferred into the general category of adult workers; however, the males would become the predominant group. The dominance of the males was rooted in established social custom and law. Women were excluded from the most skilled occupations. The average wage for skilled men exceeded the earnings for skilled women, just as the average wage for unskilled men exceeded that for unskilled women.[30] Although male weavers in the Alamance Mill earned more than female weavers under a uniform piece-rate system, the econometric study of the payroll data presented in Chapter 2 also provides evidence of sex discrimination in wages. Furthermore, the avowed inferiority of women was formalized in legal inequities.[31]

The employment of children gradually emerged as a controversial issue during the late nineteenth century. Within the mill community, opposition to the practice of child labor initially was directed against the lazy, irresponsible fathers who refused to work daily because they were able to live off the toil of their children. These parents were derisively labeled the "tin-bucket toters"; their only work was simply to carry a metal lunchpail to the children at the mill at noontime. Proposals to strengthen the enforcement of vagrancy laws, rather than child labor restrictions, were advanced to deal with the fathers who shirked their financial responsibility to their families. "The best measure that could be adopted for the betterment of the conditions of the laboring class (women and children especially) would be a revision of the vagrancy act, so that the class of men who put their wives and children in cotton mills and live in ease upon the fruits of their labor could be placed on the chain-gang."[32]

A mill operative assigned to beaming room work in Randolph County, North Carolina, expressed strong opposition to child labor in 1891. As he was a homeowner with no children between the ages of 6 and 21, he would not be considered a typical operative. He asserted that "the confinement in the factories is so severe on the children that they grow up a delicate, dwarfish people. I expect that the capitalists would kick against such laws, because it would deprive them of a great quantity of cheap labor, but our legislators should bear in mind that all of the laws should not be in favor of capital."[33]

During the 1880s manufacturers began expressing their preferences not to hire very young workers. One mill reported that "We employ no child under 12 that cannot read and write."[34] Similar comments proliferated in annual reports of the North Carolina Bureau of Labor. As time passed, the preferred minimum age that manufacturers cited tended to increase, ranging from 10 to 15 years of age. One dimension of this development was an increasing recognition of the costliness of this supposed "cheap labor." Mill management maintained that children, especially uneducated children, were careless, inattentive, and destructive. Their workmanship tended to be inferior. Since young children generally received the same rate of pay as older youths or adults for identical tasks, more mature workers were favored for a given job. Typical comments by manufacturers included: "We find it more profitable to work older hands at higher prices, as an older boy or girl can see the importance of keeping their work in nice order."[35] Also, "any man who knows anything about the mill business knows that children are naturally destructive and make a good deal more waste than grown people, consequently children are the most costly help a mill can employ."[36]

Where workers in their late teens or adulthood directly competed with the children, it is undoubtedly true that the older workers were generally more productive. However, the continuing existence of a pool of potential child workers would serve to depress the general level of wages, holding down labor costs.

For specific jobs held only by children, such as doffing, the withdrawal of children would mean the substitution of more expensive adult labor to perform quite simple functions. There is an important qualitative difference between the tendency to reduce voluntarily the number of child workers and the virtual elimination of all the members of the corps of child workers.

The growing reluctance to hire children can be traced to changes in output and worker requirements, recognition of the costliness of child labor, and the maturation of the industry. One important transformation in the southern cotton textile industry was the shift toward greater integration of spinning and weaving activities which resulted in changes in the desired composition of the workforce.

Technological developments during the postbellum period facilitated the absorption of the young unskilled workforce into textile production. The ring spindle supplanted the mule spinning process prevalent in New England. It took less skill to tend ring spindles than mule spindles; therefore, the ring was better adapted to the available southern workforce. Spinning was a typical entry-level position involving light but routine work. The basic operations of rapid splicing of broken ends could be quickly learned by a young girl. A novice worker could be assigned the responsibility of tending two sides of 104 spindles each, and within several weeks, acquire sufficient skill to operate four or six sides.

Weaving and spinning activities were only gradually integrated in the South, particularly in North Carolina. Many mills, especially the smaller establishments, produced only yarn. For example, the Monroe Mill in North Carolina, incorporated in 1895, had no looms as late as 1905. However, by 1907, the mill had installed 150 looms and had doubled the available horsepower with no increase in spindleage capacity.[37] The ratio of spindles to looms in North Carolina declined from 1880 to 1899 as indicated in Table 3-3, reflecting the shift toward greater emphasis on woven cloth.

Spinning operations afforded more opportunity for the employment of young children than the weaving activities. The greater demands for strength and maturity of the weaving occupation effectively limited this job category to the older, responsible workers. Therefore, the trend toward an increased pro-

Table 3-3. Ratio of Spindles to Looms

		Integrated Mills Only	
Year	All Mills in Alamance County	Alamance County	North Carolina
1880	43.1	38.0	51.0
1899	18.9	17.7	27.0

Source: Calculated from data in North Carolina Bureau of Labor Statistics, *Annual Report*, 1887 (Raleigh: State Printer and Binder, 1887), pp. 139, 144; North Carolina Bureau of Labor and Printing, *Annual Report*, 1899 (Raleigh: State Printer and Binder, 1900), p. 212; and Ben F. Lemert, *The Cotton Textile Industry of the Southern Appalachian Piedmont* (Chapel Hill: University of North Carolina Press, 1933), p. 121.

portion of woven cloth in total output would be accompanied by a declining proportion of children in the workforce. The data included in Table 3-4 indicate that a higher proportion of children was employed in spinning mills than in integrated mills. In North Carolina in 1909, 35.6 percent of all spinners were children, but only 5.2 percent of all weavers were under age 16.[38] Hence, although the pattern of worker incentives was designed to attract whole families, relatively more mature workers and fewer children were necessary in the rapidly expanding weaving operations than had been required in the spinning room.

Table 3-4. Child Workers in North Carolina Textile Mills

Year		Percentage Children	
Proportion Children under Age 14 in 16 Mills			
1891	Mills with spinning only	16	(7 mills, 299 employees)
	Mills with spinning and weaving	12	(9 mills, 787 employees)
Proportion Children under Age 12 in 13 Counties			
1903	Mills with spinning only	5	(5 counties, 1447 employees)
	Mills with spinning and weaving	2	(8 counties, 15,012 employees)

Source: Computed from data included in North Carolina Bureau of Labor and Statistics, *Annual Report*, 1891 (Raleigh: State Printer and Binder, 1891), pp. 126–127, and N.C. Bureau of Labor and Printing, *Annual Report*, 1903 (Raleigh: State Printer and Binder, 1904), pp. 108–109.

The composition of output was further modified as the quality of output was successively upgraded. Within a product line, quality control could be improved by selectively eliminating the workers most frequently found responsible for flawed materials. Since young children were judged the group most likely to produce faults in the output, this would lead to the gradual reduction in dependence on children in future hiring decisions. As the fineness rating or grade of output was increased, the skill and training required became greater. As one mill representative stated in 1891, "We do not employ children, because ours must be as near as possible skilled workmen, and we have found children very unsatisfactory."[39] Mill managers believed that it took an inordinate outlay of resources to socialize or acclimate very young, immature children to the work environment and to train them specifically in machine tending. Hence, child labor was considered to be relatively expensive.

Although the mill officials claimed that children provided unduly costly labor services, they supported the continuation of the practice of family labor. Mill policies maintained or preserved the family labor system. The housing system, recruitment activities, and mill regulations requiring work by all but the youngest family members represented policies that served to perpetuate the family labor system. For example, the following rule was posted in a South Carolina mill in 1904: "All children, members of a family above twelve years of age, shall work regularly in the mill and shall not be excused from service therein without the consent of the superintendent for good cause."[40] An explanation for the apparent paradox is found in the heterogeneous labor requirements of the mill.

Although textile production generally demanded relatively low skill levels on average, labor input requirements were not all homogeneous. Some occupations demanded skill, sobriety, and steady work habits, all characteristics of a primary workforce. A stable dependable workforce was essential for efficient performance within this category of occupations. Other occupations allowed for greater variability in worker reliability and discipline.

During the early years of the rapid expansion of the industry, an adequate core group of experienced primary workers was absent. Although mill managers first sought to hire the mature, responsible head-of-household, they were able to negotiate the purchase of the labor services of the family as a package or tied sale. Hence, although women and children may have been relatively productive on the farm, the wage commanded by any one family member was often quite low, provided that total family income was sufficient to induce the family to relocate to the mill village. The family labor system was a response to the heterogeneous labor needs of cotton textile production. As the various tasks in the factory demanded a range of skill levels or abilities, job opportunities were not limited to mature adult operatives. There were some tasks for which children were deemed suitable. The mill then was responsible for matching the heterogeneous members of the family with the heterogeneous jobs in the mill; that is, the firm matched worker attributes with jobs. By offering incentives designed to attract whole families, the mills were able to attract both the mature primary workers and the more casual workers, and moreover, could pay them a lower wage than would have been necessary had the mill refused employment to other family members.[41]

In recruiting new workers, the mill managers wished to sort out the most productive workers from the labor queue to fill the primary jobs. However, as a condition of accepting employment, the parents may have steadfastly insisted that their children also be given employment. Typical comments by manufacturers include the following:

> We think the labor of children under 15 years of age is not profitable to mill owners, but their parents force them on us; if we refuse to work them, they (the parents) say they will go to some other mill.[42]

> Their parents often plead with us to take them [the children] with the plea that they must have them work . . . consequently in many cases we are almost compelled to take them, but we find it more profitable to work older hands at higher prices.[43]

and

> We do not want to work children under twelve years of age—resist it all we can—but when a mother brings an eleven-year-old boy to us and pleads that school is over for the year and she cannot look after her boy, that he roams the street contrary to her wishes, goes to the river with other boys, and she cannot keep up with him, and

> he wants work in the mill, and begs us to take him as he is better off
> in the mill under control than out of it, what are we to do? . . . Mills
> do not want them but work them as a charity in many cases.[44]

That the mills were willing to accede to the demands of the
parents does not imply that workers in general had substantial bargaining power which they could wield over the mill.
Quite the contrary. Worker consciousness and union participation were generally weak.[45] First of all, the testimony of manufacturers was to some extent self-serving, absolving the mills of
the social or moral responsibility for forcing children to work.
More importantly, the practice of child labor must be considered with respect to the job bargaining process. In order to
attract the workers, mill management offered a combination
package of incentives, including both the wage and working
conditions. In a strategic bargaining maneuver, the mill managers conveyed the impression that they had yielded to parental
pressure; but in so doing, the mill was effectively responding
to the heterogeneous labor input requirements of cotton textile
production. By gradually increasing the minimum acceptable
age, the mill retained the flexibility of tapping the labor services
of several family members yet was able to alter the relative proportions of mature and young workers.

Alternatively, the desire to assure the continuing availability
of a mature labor force may have provided the rationale for
hiring the child as well as the parent. It was deemed essential
to begin the training and socialization process at an early age in
order to develop a superior workforce for the future operations
of the firm. As one manufacturer commented:

> At twelve they must begin at the same point as at eleven, with chances
> of advancing no faster, but with the chances of being an obedient
> and desirable operative greatly diminished.[46]

Thus, one objective of hiring the youngest workers was to initiate the child to the factory environment at an early age. Further,
the employed parent would provide a stabilizing influence over
his offspring in the mill, economizing on supervisory costs.

On the supply side of the labor market, the changing composition of the textile workforce and the declining proportion of
child workers are not surprising in light of the time path of

the industry. The workforce of 1870 had a much larger fraction of very young workers than was found in 1900. When adult earnings tended to rise, labor force participation rates of younger children tended to decline. The age of first entry into the labor force tended to increase with the rise of family incomes. Moreover, many of the young workers of the 1880s and early 1890s remained employed in the cotton textile industry on into their adulthood, providing a pool of mature, experienced workers in 1900. In contrast, although there had been a small boom in textile mill activity in the South during the 1840s, there was no such core group of comparable size available in 1870. The existence of the larger pool of mature mill workers in 1900 diminished the incentive to fill the ranks of operatives with "raw recruits," or families transferred directly from the farm sector. With variations in the number of families recruited, observed changes in the age structure of the workforce would be expected, abstracting from the changes in the typical age structure of new workers.

The supply side effect of increased availability of mature workers was reinforced by the changing age distribution of the population. There was a tendency toward the aging of the population after 1890, with the proportion of the total accounted for by children and teenagers declining in importance. The proportion of the population under the age of 15 declined in the South Atlantic region from 40 percent in 1890 to 38 percent in 1910.[47] Furthermore, the proportions of the population in two prime working age groups, ages 20 to 29 and 30 to 44, had both increased by 1910 as shown in Table 3-5. The aging of the population coincided with the changing composition of the labor force, assuming no change in age-specific labor force participation rates.

The enactment of legal prohibitions against child labor was widely opposed in spite of the gradually rising resistance to the extensive employment of children.[48] The Southerner has long been characterized as a fiercely independent individual, suspicious of outside interference in his personal affairs.[49] The decisions regarding family welfare and the appropriateness of employment of the offspring were considered the inalienable prerogative of the parent. Any encroachment upon this power, such as child labor restrictions, was thus strongly resented.

Table 3-5. Composition of the Southern Population (percentages)

Age	1870	1890	1910
0–4	15.6	14.1	13.8
5–19	37.8	38.9	35.0
20–29	17.7	16.6	18.1
30–44	15.6	16.3	17.5
45–64	10.7	11.0	12.2
65 +	2.6	3.1	3.4

Source: Warren S. Thompson and P. K. Whelpton, *Population Trends in the United States,* Demographic Monographs, vol. 9 (New York: McGraw-Hill Book Company, 1933; reprint ed., New York: Gordon and Breach Science Publishers, 1969), p. 121.

Therefore, labor restrictions were opposed on the basis of a broad, fundamental principle of individual freedom of determination as well as the specific concern of the abolition of child labor.

The laissez-faire attitude was also shared by the manufacturers. Consistent with their paternalistic stance, the manufacturers declared they should be able to exercise freely their own discretion in determining who should be able to work in the mill. The viewpoint was expressed by one manager: "I see no chance to improve the condition of wage-earners over what they now enjoy except that the Legislature let them alone to follow their avocations without disturbance. . . . They are fully able to take care of themselves and will do so if let alone."[50] The above statement, of course, tacitly assumed that the operatives would remain under the direction and guidance of the paternalistic mill manager. As an official of a North Carolina mill claimed, "Who is the laborer's true friend? The manufacturer, of course."[51]

Manufacturers also believed that all efforts should initially be concentrated upon firmly establishing the foundation of the cotton textile industry in the South. A strong base would assure the continuing viability of the nascent industry. Only after the major industry was successfully permanently planted in the South should attention be redirected toward furthering specific goals of social betterment.[52] The overall benefits to be derived from the industry were so great, and as everything could not be accomplished immediately, it was considered rational to delay social reform until the "infant industry" had reached self-sustaining maturity. The gradualist approach, which parallels the laissez-faire position, was based upon the belief that the process of free market interaction would ultimately yield the socially desirable outcome, given sufficient adjustment time.

Undoubtedly the mill managers were aware of the mounting concern over the issue of children working long hours six days a week in a mill. Acting as if they anticipated the rising criticism of child labor, the manufacturers attempted to delay the implementation of mandatory regulations. More importantly, the mill managers feared that the adoption of restrictive child labor legislation would establish a precedent for further labor legislation. Despite the lower skill level of southern workers in comparison with New England laborers, the southern manufacturers remained convinced that southern labor was relatively cheap. Labor restrictions would reduce the regional labor cost differential, and it was claimed that this would threaten the viability of the infant industry. "If we have no advantages in the South over new England mills they will, on account of their location, have an advantage over the mills in the South."[53]

One important aspect of the increasing restrictions on child labor was school attendance. Education in the mill village was the main alternative activity to factory employment for children of mill families. The mill managers assumed additional leverage in the job bargaining process with regard to increasing the minimum working age when schools were made available for the mill village children. More importantly, the provision of schooling for the children provided both a signaling mechanism for the screening of mature job applicants and a training center for developing desirable worker skills and traits. The following chapter examines the interaction between schooling and the family labor system in the southern cotton mill village.

4

Schooling in the Mill Villages

Southern textile mills devoted substantial resources to the establishment and support of schools within the mill communities. Investment in education by mill management was a function of the demand for an efficient workforce. Management's provision of schooling was not simply an act of disinterested altruism or beneficence but was an activity consistent with profit-maximizing behavior. The provision of schooling was a response to the employment of an inexperienced workforce recently transferred from the agricultural sector. Mill schools served a critical function in both the initial hiring process and in the continuing development or training of the workforce. Nevertheless, despite the financial commitment of mill managers to schools, the mill village parents did not always choose to send their children to school. The apparently indifferent attitude of workers toward schooling is explained by the high cost to the family and the relatively low perceived private benefits.

The southern states trailed significantly behind the New England states in public expenditures for schooling, as suggested by the data presented in Table 4-1.

Although textile manufacturers in both New England and the South valued educated workers, the extent and form of the

Table 4-1. Quality of Schools: Length of School Term and Expenditures per Pupil

	Average Length of School Term (in days)			
	1879–1880	1888–1890	1899–1900	1907–1908
United States	130.3	134.7	144.3	154.1
Massachusetts	177	177	189	188
North Carolina	50	59.3	70.5	98.3
South Carolina	70	69.6	88.4	95.5

Total Expenditure Per Pupil (Based on Average Attendance) 1907–1908	
Massachusetts	$43.12
North Carolina	$ 9.06
South Carolina	$ 6.90

Source: U.S. Commission of Education, *Annual Report*, 1909, vol 2: 609–617.

participation of the mills in the educational process differed greatly in the two regions. In Massachusetts during the nineteenth century, the mill officials had given political support to the extension of common schools through public taxation.[1] In contrast, in the South during the postbellum period, the mills were unable to rely exclusively upon the state to provide an adequate schooling system.[2] Hence, southern mills were much more directly involved in both the financing and operation of the schools. The participation of the New England mills and southern mills in the schooling process was compared in a 1907 Senate report on the cotton textile industry:

> In the education of the cotton-mill children the individual mill owner in the New England states . . . plays but a small part. In those States a well-grounded public-school sentiment and a well-established public-school system antedated the extensive development of the cotton industry. The employer, being freed by the State from any responsibility for the education of the children of the people from whom he draws his labor supply, turns any philanthropic plans he may have into other channels.

> On the other hand, in Virginia, North Carolina, South Carolina, Georgia, Alabama, and Mississippi the individual mill owner plays a very important part in connection with the common-school systems. . . . [Many of the cotton mill schools were] built, equipped,

and almost entirely supported and controlled by the cotton-mill cor-
porations in towns entirely made up of cotton-mill people. These
schools are peculiar to the South and to the cotton industry in the
South.[3]

Given the lack of a comprehensive public school system,
southern textile mills subsidized mill town schools. Although
many mill schools were wholly financed by the mill, frequently
mill funds supplemented local tax appropriations. Often a mill
would incur all initial costs of establishing and administering a
school. If the surrounding community was already serviced by a
local school district when the mill was founded, perhaps the mill
management would construct a school house more conveniently
located for mill village residents. Management then continued
to subsidize the cost of teachers' salaries, school equipment, and
supplies.

A survey of 77 mills constructed in North Carolina between
1880 and 1900 found that 13 schools were newly established
by the respective mill; 56 mills were located within existing
school system jurisdictions, with many of these mills opening
new schoolhouses within the mill village boundaries; 3 schools
were established at a later date by the respective mill; and 5
schools were later started by local government.[4] In another survey of 41 mills in North Carolina in 1890, mill managers were
asked if there were good educational facilities for mill village
residents. The responses were: yes (32), very good (2), fairly
good (3), fair (1), and no (3).[5]

It was generally accepted that, on average, mill school facilities
were superior in quality to southern rural schools and compared
favorably with town schools. The length of the school term,
one indicator of the financial commitment to and the quality
of schools, tended to be greater in counties in which mills were
located. In a sample of 74 counties in North Carolina in 1880,
the mean number of weeks of school per year was 11.65 in mill
counties but only 9.50 for non-mill counties.[6] Further, in 1913
in Gastonia, North Carolina, the length of the school term for
city and mill schools was 8 months but only 5 months in the
rural schools.[7]

To secure and train a labor force, mill managers pursued policies that incorporated the dual personnel functions of recruitment of workers and on-going labor development programs.
Mill schools served both functions, offering an effective induce-

ment to attract high-quality workers and thereafter performing a critical role in supplying a continuing stream of educated, disciplined workers to the mill.[8]

With the rapid growth of the cotton textile industry during the postbellum period, mill managers found it necessary to employ workers recently recruited from southern farms. Mill managers were naturally interested in seeking out the best workers from the available adult labor pool. A. Michael Spence has analyzed the role of education as a signal.[9] The employer may use schooling as an indicator of worker quality when estimating how productive an individual worker is likely to be. Application of the signaling model to the family labor system in the textile industry requires some modification. Using literacy directly as a criterion or qualification for employment would have sorted out too few potential workers. From the employer's perspective, a parent's desire for education for his children was considered an indicator of the likelihood that the parent was a worker of relatively high productivity, even if the parent were himself illiterate. Harriet Herring has observed that mill management, by offering good schools for the children:

> hoped to attract a steadier, soberer, more hardworking class of people, the kind of men who were willing to work themselves instead of sending their wives and children to the mill while they loafed at the store.[10]

Parents who recognized the importance of schooling for their children would actively search out mills providing the best school facilities. The mills offering good schools would thereby attract a relatively high proportion of the group of parents considered to be the most able workers. This would increase the perceived probability that the workers within the labor queue facing the mill would on average be superior to the average quality of workers in the aggregate labor supply, even if they did not themselves have high educational attainments. Herring further observed that "mills indifferent to school facilities have been obliged to be satisfied with the poorest type of people."[11] Hence, the provision of village schools represented an effective self-selection screening mechanism in the recruitment process.

The mill schools thus served to attract the desirable mature primary workers. Furthermore, the mills continued to promote the development of a skilled, disciplined workforce through the education of the children. The continuing contribution of education within the company towns may best be understood with reference to the family labor system and mill village paternalism. As the school curriculum was largely devoted to general topics such as the "Three R's," it would apparently seem that the training was of a quite general nature. The children could leave the mill village shortly upon completion of schooling, and the mill would then be unable to recoup the cost of this investment by increased productivity of the individual. Therefore, it may be argued that underwriting the cost of schooling was an extremely risky venture and an inordinately expensive method of acquiring a literate adult workforce. However, the system of family labor and mill village residence served to increase the probability that a child educated in the mill village school would eventually work in the mill.

Gary Becker has argued that forces that limit labor mobility or augment monopsony power increase the specific qualities of a training program.[12] The skills from schooling would be less easily transferred to another firm when barriers to the free movement of workers existed. In a mill community, the cotton mill was the chief or sole employer, implying some degree of monopsony power. The whole welfare village concept was designed to stabilize the workforce and increase the average tenure of workers. The family labor system strengthened the forces of labor immobility. Usually a mill was moderately successful in retaining a core population over an extended period of time. It would be expected that, upon completion of schooling, the children from the core group of families would also enter the mill. Mill regulations frequently required that children over a minimum age provide their labor services to the mill as a condition of continuing employment of the older family members. If workers and their families would remain at the mill for a long period, the real gains from training could be captured over a longer time horizon, thereby increasing the willingness of a firm to invest in a training or schooling program.

The persistence of a core group of workers was suggested by the data presented in Chapter 2 for the Alamance Mill workforce. According to the housing ledger for the Alamance Mill, of the 24 company dwellings, 13 of the homes were rented to heads of households in 1908 whose families remained in the mill village at least until 1920.[13]

One traditional argument advanced in support of education of the workers was the increasing demand for skilled workers to improve the quality of output. Managers frequently commented on the shortage of educated, skilled, experienced operatives as a constraint on the movement into higher grades of textile output. A mill owner wrote in a letter: "the spinning and weaving done [in southern cotton mills] are both of the simplest kind. . . . there is vast room for improvement yet if we can develop by education and training a knowledge of how to do it."[14] With education, workers tend to adapt more easily to a changing work process and are less resistant to the introduction of new techniques.[15] To improve the quality of the mill's output, higher skills and education were demanded at several phases of the production process. The weaving of fine cloth required more skilled weavers and also greater attention to the production of finer yarns. As the shift to a finer quality of output did not involve simply the addition of a final finishing activity but the upgrading of several successive intermediate activities, the change in output demanded that a sizable proportion of the workforce be educated.

A variant of the argument linking education and output quality relates to the need for educated and skilled supervisors and managers. A change in the composition of output required technical expertise and knowledge to arrange the necessary machine adjustments and reallocation of personnel. An incompetent superintendent "has been known to stop his whole mill while he figured out how he could remedy a slight defect in the gearing."[16] Finis Welch has analyzed the allocative effect of schooling. Education enhances the ability to evaluate and respond effectively to changing information and technology.[17] Therefore, in a dynamic context, education of managers facilitated innovation, and hence, augmented worker productivity.

In addition to the contribution of education in teaching technical expertise and signaling worker information, mill village schools played a central role in developing noncognitive or affective skills. Institutions, such as the family, schools, and churches, are fundamental to the transmission of acceptable social values and patterns of behavior. Alexander Field has documented the impetus for the common school movement in mid-nineteenth century industrial Massachusetts arising from the perceived need for a socialization process given the waning strength of traditional institutions such as the family and the church.[18]

In contrast, the schools in southern mill villages represented complements to strong family units and the church, not substitutes. The family labor system provided the means for a family unit to remain intact in the manufacturing community. Family labor and the helper system tended to preserve traditional authoritative roles within the family in the mill. In addition, the church retained its influence as a spiritual force in the villages, providing a powerful mechanism for inculcating acceptable beliefs and attitudes. As the mill owners financially supported the churches, the pastors were under their sway and therefore espoused behavior sympathetic to the needs of management. According to Herring:

> Then it must be remembered that the clergymen of the denominations most active in mill villages naturally believe and preach doctrines which would be acceptable in the main to a capitalistic employer—a gospel of work, of gratitude for present blessings, and of patience with economic and social maladjustment as temporal and outside the sphere of religious concern. . . .[19]

The schools and the churches instilled in the workers a set of social norms conducive to improved productivity in the factory setting. As the workforce was largely composed of workers who had migrated from a relatively sparsely populated rural sector, the social tensions introduced by movement into a mill village and a new work environment were particularly strong. The degree of independence and individual control over the production process had been much greater on the farm than in the factory. The workers, therefore, had to become accustomed to the regimentation and discipline demanded by the mill routine. Punctuality, regularity of attendance, reliability, attentiveness, respect for authority, and ambition were all traits the mill managers wished to foster among the mill village population. Because the flow of production proceeded more smoothly with a disciplined workforce, the mill managers had incentive to invest resources in socializing activities to decrease the cost of production.

Numerous comments by manufacturers attest to the perceived socialization function of mill schools. The president of a North Carolina mill stated that "we feel very proud of our mill school; the principal told me she never saw better behaved children."[20] Another mill official observed that "children who are educated become more valuable labor and are less destructive of property."[21] Further, "increased education would undoubtedly mean increased morality."[22] The emphasis on behavior training and modification is indicated by the official lesson plans for schools in Reidsville, North Carolina, in 1894 which dictated that "a systematic course of training should be given in morals and manners, embracing the subjects of respectfulness . . . honesty . . . truthfulness . . . reverence &c."[23] Moreover, it was believed that education tended to increase the strength of management authority. A docile, pliable worker was more easily controlled and supervised. One cotton textile manufacturer opined: "We find educated labor is much more satisfactory; they have fewer prejudices, [are] more easily satisfied and can adjust themselves to suit emergencies understandingly."[24]

Exhortations against the evils of the consumption of alcohol were frequently included in the school lesson plans. Alcoholism and intoxication on the job were recognized as serious industrial problems.[25] The paternalistic teachings against intemperance were therefore consistent with the self-interest of management, not simply a selfless concern for the health and welfare of the mill village residents.

Schools performed a custodial or child care function when both parents were employed in the mill, keeping children occupied and away from the temptations of the street life. Idleness among youths was thought to promote laziness rather than the more desirable traits of hard work and industriousness. Furthermore, idleness was considered a vice that could lead to more dissolute behavior. Education, however, was perceived to be an effective deterrent to crime. One manager expressed the following viewpoint: "Spend more money on our schools and less on our penitentiaries, and sooner or later we shall have less call for expenditures on the penitentiaries, if we give an education that educates."[26]

Samuel Bowles and Herbert Gintis have argued that the American education system effectively filters people into the hierarchical base of the capitalist structure. Hence, the schools help to perpetuate the prevailing social and economic order of the capitalist system. Simply stated, "schools produce workers."[27] That the mill village school system functioned in this way is suggested by the insistence of some managers that schooling beyond the common school level was inappropriate or undesirable. The elementary school was considered sufficient for developing skills and work traits appropriate to operatives in the factory hierarchy. The prevailing view was that some schooling was desirable but that too much education spoiled the worker. Of those students who went on to high school, very few ever came back to the mill to work,[28] supporting the management viewpoint that the common school level provided sufficient preparation for mill work.

Another important rationale for the presence of schools rested upon the fluctuating labor needs of the mill and the strategy of job bargaining. The early mills, which were dependent upon water power, curtailed operations when the water level was too low to generate sufficient power. There also tended to be some seasonal variation in the demand for the labor input. As the production process did not always proceed smoothly or at a regular pace, labor requirements fluctuated. Moreover, irregular attendance by some workers caused occasional deficiencies in the daily available labor force. In response to the varying labor needs, mill managers employed adult temporary or casual workers, called "spare hands." In addition, schools provided a supplementary reserve pool of labor to meet short-term surges in labor demand. During a Senate investigation of the textile industry in 1907, it was reported that "It was the custom for the overseers in the mill to send to the schoolhouse at any time of day for workers. The mill came first always, the school after."[29]

The labor requirements for a normal level of production were satisfied on a continuing basis by older family members of the mill village population. During periods of peak labor demand, additional workers were quickly drawn in from the ranks of school children. The cost of hiring these temporary workers was relatively low in comparison with recruitment outside the mill village. When labor demands again declined from the peak level, the children were released from the mill and returned to the school.

Mill managers frequently expressed their reluctance to retain young workers in the factory on a regular basis. Without the schools, parental pressure for the continuing employment of the children would have undoubtedly been more vehement. To mollify the families of desirable workers, a continuing obligation or commitment to the temporary workers nonetheless remained. The excess child workers were not summarily discharged but were transferred back to the school. Thus, the provision of schooling represented an integral part of the labor bargaining process within the context of the family labor system.

Despite the financial commitment of mill managers to schooling, a large proportion of mill workers did not avail themselves of the educational opportunities in the mill villages. In Durham County, North Carolina, the proportion of school-age children enrolled in schools was significantly lower at the mill schools than at other schools in the district. Although the average enrollment rate for the Durham school district was 71.3 percent during the 1902 school year, the corresponding proportions at the three mill schools ranged from 49.5 to 50.8 percent.[30] In 1905 it was reported that in South Carolina "the average mill town [school] has better buildings, more funds, but relatively less enrollment than the average county school."[31] In Morgantown, Burke County, North Carolina, the enrollment was higher among non-mill children than mill children in 1906. According to the school superintendent for this district, "The chief thing that causes the enrollment of white children [in Morgantown] to be so low is that from the operatives at the two cotton factories fewer than a dozen children come to school."[32] The two mills in Burke County were both spinning mills which tended to employ a relatively high proportion of youths. In a later study of Gastonia, North Carolina, similar findings were reported. In 1913, the average proportion of enrolled students in attendance was 52.8 percent for the eight mill schools; but at the central school serving the town population, the average attendance rate was 77.4 percent.[33]

In evaluating the potential net benefits of an education, the parents would consider whether a child's additional future earnings attributable to the acquisition of schooling could justify the loss of present earnings.[34] A factor of great importance to the parents' decision of the optimal level of schooling for children was the loss of the child's income. Table 3-2 presented age-earnings data for young mill workers in 1907. In the absence of minimum age restrictions imposed by company policy or statute, school attendance meant foregone earnings that could have supplemented the meager family income. Economic exigency often foreclosed the opportunity for enrollment. A mill operative in 1891 explained: "I am a widow, with three children—two boys and one girl. I am not able to send my children to school. I have to work and have them work. This is a cause of grief to me, as they are bright children, and would be smart in books if they had a chance."[35]

Furthermore, in some cases the option of school attendance was foreclosed by a requirement that the children work in the factory. Minimizing the importance of this effect, a mill official stated that "we arrange to relieve as many as possible from their work in the cotton mill to attend school, and very few are retained who desire to go."[36] In contrast, a mill employee in 1891 emphasized the importance of restrictive mill policies. Although he recognized that many parents were too poor to send their children to school, he declared that even "if they were able to send them it would be against the wishes of the managers for them to do so, as they need the children's labor in the mill."[37]

The relative importance of the foregone income in the schooling decision is suggested by the cyclical fluctuations in enrollments. During unusually bad years, enrollments would decline. After registering a fall in attendance of 2,477 white students in South Carolina for 1895, the Superintendent of Education reported that "it is, perhaps, but fair to attribute the loss this year to the extra demands of parents for the services of their children on account of the financial stringency of the year."[38] Farming was characterized by a longer seasonal slack period during which school sessions were conducted. Seasonal declines were less marked in the factory than on the farm, so mill families sacrificed potentially higher earnings if their children did not work. As family income rose over time, the withdrawal of children from labor force participation became more feasible or attractive.

During 1891 a cotton mill employee in Randolph County, North Carolina, estimated that of the 500 school-age children in the area, 340 children were unable to attend school due to work in the mill. The South Carolina Superintendent of Schools conducted a survey in 1905 of 281 parents who failed to send their children to school. The three most frequently cited responses for nonattendance involved the indirect and direct costs of schooling. The three reasons were: the parents wanted the children to work, the family could not afford to purchase suitable clothing, and the family could not afford to buy books. In a later study of the attendance reports for a school in a South Carolina mill town, the tensions that existed between school attendance and mill work were evident. During the two-week period January 1 to January 15, 1908, 23 students drawn from a classroom of 72 students, ages 6 to 16, lost a total of 223 days from school due to work in the mill.[39]

In addition to the costs incurred in the acquisition of an education, the benefits to be derived from schooling were also a crucial determinant of the schooling decision. A rise in expected lifetime earnings due to education would be positively associated with the optimal number of years of schooling. However, many families believed that the benefits did not outweigh the costs.

The connection between schooling, productivity, and earnings was often too vague and hazy. As discussed above, schools tended to concentrate on the "Three R's" and on activities that developed social values. The curriculum incorporated little in the way of vocational training, although influential educators frequently recommended greater attention to this area. The lack of vocational studies is important to the analysis of supply and demand conditions in two ways. First, it gives strength to the argument that the socialization function was more important than the specific technical skills taught in schools. Second, the relevance of schooling to earning a livelihood would have been questionable to already skeptical or indifferent parents. A more practical curriculum would have enhanced their perception of the potential benefits to be derived from schooling. A mill employee remarked that mill students "need in their day and night schools books that treat of textile manufacturing; they need when studying arithmetic to be taught the various calculations necessary in making changes in mills."[40]

With regard to expected future incremental income gains, the occupational outlook or aspirations of youths in the mill village was central to the schooling decision. In retrospect, mill work became almost an "hereditary occupation." Therefore, children born and raised in the mill village perhaps felt destined to remain as mill operatives in their adulthood. Some parents maintained that as they had managed to get by well enough without schooling so also could their children.[41] Many families perhaps were simply resigned to the fact that their children would probably wind up in the mill anyway, and they therefore wondered why they should bother to send their children to school. Moreover, the primary means of entry for most relatively skilled or supervisory positions was "up through the ranks." One of the most highly paid individuals at the Alamance Mill was illiterate, for example. Even as late as 1930, the entry jobs for at least 29 cotton mill managers of a survey group of 50 managers were at the unskilled level: sweeper (25 cases), spinning room helper (3 cases), and bobbin boy (1 case). Of this group of 50 mangers, 38 percent had begun work between the ages of 7 and 11, and 46 percent of the total had started before the age of 14.[42]

Further, as shown in Table 2-7, the estimation of the earnings functions for the Alamance Mill did not reveal a significant positive relationship between individual earnings and literacy, when adjustments were made for experience, sex, and age. Similar results were obtained by Harold Luft and Thomas Dublin in their studies of mid-nineteenth century Lowell millworkers. Luft observed that piece-rate productivity data exhibited no significant statistical relationship between individual worker productivity and literacy. Dublin also found no evidence that education significantly affected either productivity or daily earnings. However, there may yet have been a private return to literacy not captured by the regressions for the Alamance Mill payroll. In a recent study of a large cross-sectional sample of cotton textile workers in the United States in 1907, Claudia Goldin and Donald Parsons have estimated that annual income tended to rise 2 percent with each year of schooling.[43]

Of course, the importance of movement "up through the ranks" did not preclude the possibility that education increased the probability that a given individual would attain the status of a relatively high-paying occupation. Rather, it suggests that schooling may have been considered an unnecessary prerequisite to some of the better paying jobs. If movement up the ranks provided a feasible path, then perhaps a youth's time was better spent in working as a doffer at the foot of a job ladder rather than undertaking the costly, uncertain route of schooling which postponed work experience.

In summary, the commitment to schooling may be interpreted as a response by the mill managers to the need to secure an industrial workforce from within an agricultural community. The schools played a critical role in both the initial recruitment process and also in the on-going development or training of workers. By offering superior school facilities, mill managers expected initially to attract job applicants comprised of a relatively high proportion of the workers thought to be most productive on average. The provision of a high-quality school provided management with a self-selection signaling device for screening workers drawn from the farm sector. Further, the schools played an essential role in the continuing development of the workforce by promoting desirable worker traits and acceptable patterns of behavior. Notwithstanding, attendance rates at mill schools tended to be low because families needed income from their children's labor and saw little short- or long-term benefit in schooling.

Given the importance of the interrelationship between the pattern of labor organization and the incentives for the provision of schooling, this research offers a different perspective on the analysis presented by Field regarding the role of manufacturers in supporting education. In Massachusetts, manufacturers' involvement in the education process was limited primarily to political support of the expansion of the school system through increased public taxation, whereas in the South the mill managers were much more directly involved in all facets of the actual operations of the schools.

In the postbellum southern textile industry, the influence of the comprehensive welfare system in promoting worker stability tended to transform the character of the schooling activity from general to specific in nature. If a broad definition of investment in human capital is assumed, then the development of an adaptable, disciplined, responsive workforce through the schooling process represented augmentation of human capital.

5

The Mill Families

The family labor system represents a significant extension of the traditional sphere of the family as the relevant decision-making unit. In the southern textile town experience, the firm interacted with the family as a whole, not with the individual, during the job bargaining process.

Demographers have frequently hypothesized that industrial families tend to have fewer children than their agrarian counterparts. This pattern is inferred from the observed fertility differential between the urban and rural sector, with the movement to the city being associated with a decline in family size.[1] As the growth of industry is typically associated with the concentration of population in industrial centers, one would therefore expect that the rise in manufacturing would be accompanied by a drop in fertility and a decline in family size. In contrast, the postbellum southern cotton mill village tended to gather together relatively large families in the industrial community.

The family labor system exerted a selective bias toward households with several members. New workers were selectively drawn from the southern farm sector, a group with generally high fertility. Children provided both direct satisfaction to their parents, as well as indirect satisfaction deriving from the value of their labor services rendered on the farm. When alternative non-farm employment opportunities for the families opened up in the cotton mills, the labor recruitment policies were structured by management so as to induce the flow of relatively large families to the mill villages. A large number of children would increase the probability that a family would secure employment in the mill. Furthermore, the textile industry remained much more decentralized in the South than in New England. Many mills were located in small piedmont towns and villages rather than in large cities with high population densities as in Massachusetts.[2]

During the past few decades, economists have developed formal models of the family as a social and economic institution. It may be helpful to approach the southern cotton textile mill family by considering how this household unit differed from that suggested by the assumptions embodied in some of the recent models. For this purpose, the model formulated by Robert Willis, which analyzes the basic nuclear family with both parents present in the home, is representative.[3] In the model developed by Willis, decisions about fertility, numbers of children, and the wife's labor force participation are made early in the marriage and are based on consideration of the best use of the parents' time and resources. As the father's time is productive only in the marketplace by assumption, he will work full time in remunerative employment. The lifetime labor supply of the female parent is accordingly a choice variable of the model. It is assumed that children are not engaged in remunerative employment. The outcome yields an efficient allocation of limited resources between the production of child services and other sources of satisfaction.

However, there are serious limitations in applying Willis' model to the study of family size in the southern cotton mill village. In his model, the number of children is a variable to be determined at the outset of marriage simultaneously with the decision as to the best use of each parent's time. In contrast, in the mill village the time allocation decision was altered by the opportunity for employment of children. More importantly, for many mill families, the fertility decision was made before the move to the mill village. In a sense, fertility choice was then no longer the crucial variable in determining family size among the mill workers. Rather, we should investigate the forces leading to the selective migration of families who already had relatively large numbers of children as well as the influences within the mill village that reinforced the desirability of a large family.

In the cotton mill villages, family size tended to be large, suggestive of a population that was not extensively practicing family limitation. The lack of widely disseminated contraceptive information could account for the failure to control fertility. Alternatively, the parents could have chosen intentionally not to contracept. Given the possibility of remunerative employment of the children, the optimal number of offspring may have exceeded the expected number of children under conditions of natural fertility. If the marginal benefit of children exceeded the marginal cost of children over the full range of natural fertility, then the parents would not consider family limitation to be worthwhile.

Unrestricted fertility would be predicted from the possibilities for the employment of children when the income the parents received from their children exceeded rearing costs. Appendix B shows this prediction formally for a case in which children's only value to parents is their financial contribution. If children also directly increase their parents' happiness, this result is reinforced. This has two implications: (1) a couple with a preference for large families or an aversion to birth control (on moral, religious, or other grounds) would be induced to migrate into economic regions with a family labor system; and (2) families in the mill villages would not practice family limitation.

In contrast to the early nineteenth century cotton mills in Lowell, Massachusetts, the postbellum southern textile mills relied heavily upon the family labor system, employing several members of any given household.[4] The hiring practices of the southern mills provided incentive for large families to migrate to the mill towns and influenced the fertility decision of potential workers. A prominent feature of the labor supply process for our purposes is the extensive employment of child labor. The underlying motivation for having children is not explored in depth by Willis. Although the financial contribution of the youthful members of the family would represent an indirect source of satisfaction through the provision of market or purchased goods, Willis dismissed this role. The data for his study were derived from a sample of American families in 1960. By 1960, the proportion of total family income furnished by the earnings of children was minimal. However, as this was not the case in the postbellum South, we must integrate this consideration into our analysis of the cotton mill families. At that time, the children frequently provided a significant fraction of the total family income. For single-parent families or for families headed by a disabled parent, it was not uncommon for the wages of the children to account for a significant portion of the family income stream. Although children required that substantial resources be expended during their early maturation and development, they would eventually sell their labor services and increase the flow of market goods to the family.

The postbellum southern cotton textile mill family is not accurately characterized as a nuclear family unit with the father engaged full time in the labor force. A large segment of the labor force was composed of widows and their children. In the Manuscript Census of 1880 for Melville Township in Alamance County, there were 39 household units recorded in which at least one family member was a cotton textile mill worker. In 17 of these homes with children less than 20 years of age, the head-of-household was a widow or married woman with no spouse present. Also, in a 1907 sample of 325 young operatives ages 14 to 15 who worked in North Carolina cotton mills, 11.7 percent (38 children) were the children of widows. In South Carolina the proportion was even higher. From a total of 279 children, 17.6 percent (49 children) were the children of widows.[5]

The time allocation decision for a household headed by a single parent was fundamentally different from that of the two-parent nuclear family. Without the flow of income earned by the father, the full burden of providing even the barest means of subsistence fell directly upon the remaining family members. Consequently, either the mother or children had to obtain remunerative employment simply to support the family, given the lack of adequate social welfare programs. This did not necessarily dictate that the mother assume the role of primary breadwinner; rather the possibility existed for the older children to enter the mill if the mother's time was occupied with child care and housekeeping activities in the home. The recent theoretical literature tends to assume the wife spends more time in child rearing than the husband. The wife is also portrayed as commanding a comparative advantage in homemaking and child care activities. However, the allocation of child-rearing responsibility must be modified for the single-parent family with several children.

Within a large young family headed by a widow, the mother may have remained in the home caring for the youngest of her children, with labor force participation thrust upon the older children. In Melville Township of Alamance County, of the 17 households with children under age 20 in which only one parent was present, in only one case did the mother work in the mill herself. In the remaining 16 cases, the mothers remained in the home engaged in full-time housekeeping or child care duties.[6] The family labor system in the factory fostered this arrangement. In the mill, siblings frequently worked in close proximity of each other, allowing a large degree of family supervision and control in the midst of the working environment. Family authority and cohesion were thus preserved, not displaced, by the mill routine and regimentation. The older sibling, working adjacent to the younger sister or brother, provided some of the necessary functions of child care, supervision, and on-the-job training, while gainfully employed. As a result, there was joint production of marketed goods and child quality. This is at variance with Willis' assumption that time devoted to labor market activity was unavailable for household production.

After all the children in the widow's family had reached either school or working age, the likelihood of the mother returning to the mill increased. This is related to the empirical observation that the probability of labor force participation and the number of children in the household are inversely related.[7] Although the children had not yet departed from the household, they had matured beyond the age of complete economic dependency. With the reduced need for childcare for the very young children, the value of the mother's time spent in the home tended to decline relative to her market wage. The practice of the "helper system" hastened this development and provides another example of joint production. Children too young or inexperienced to be hired by the mill were allowed to work as unpaid helpers to the mother. This would free the mother at an earlier date from the necessity of remaining in the home for the custodial care of children and would serve to supplement the mother's earnings if she were paid on a piece-rate basis.

It is assumed that the probability of labor force participation for the widowed mother is based on the comparison of the market wage (*W*) to the "shadow price" or value of the widow's time in the home rather than in the labor force (*W**). If *W* > *W**, there is a positive probability that the woman will work. The helper system then increases *W* and diminishes *W** as child care need not be restricted to the home setting. In addition, a child conditioned to the factory routine tended to receive higher wages than an inexperienced child when he or she was finally included on the company payroll. With a life-cycle planning horizon for the household, this would further increase the relative value of the mother's time in the mill.

Another dimension of the impact of the employment of the children upon the nuclear family relates to the incentives of the father of a two-parent household to remain in the labor force.[8] Willis assumes that since the father is unproductive in the home, he will choose to work fulltime. In contrast, some fathers of mill families engaged in casual or part-time work only. In a sample of 723 working fathers of wage-earning children under 17 in 1907, a Senate investigator found that 13.7 percent worked less than 50 percent of the year and 2.6 percent worked less than 50 days per year. In the mill village it was frequently claimed that irresponsible fathers, the "tin-bucket toters," simply took advantage of their authority to send their children into the mill, allowing themselves the luxury to laze away the day in idleness. However, such claims were likely exaggerated. The 1907 study reported that "It was found that the absolutely idle father, who contributed nothing whatever to the family support . . . was not so much in evidence as the father who 'puttered around' at odd jobs just sufficient to give him some claim to be a worker."[9]

Moreover, the early child labor legislation provided further disincentive to the father's labor force participation. Although the legal sanctions against child labor were generally mild, the force of these measures was further weakened by the inclusion of clauses providing for exceptions to the minimum age rule. Children were allowed to work legally at a younger age on the basis of family need, such as when the father was ill or disabled and unable to work. If the father were to withdraw from the labor force due to some exaggerated or feigned disability, then his children would be permitted to work. Having worked a long time on the farm, an older father may have found the transition to a new occupation in the mill difficult. Given his age, his fingers may have lacked the dexterity demanded in handling materials and machine tending. The combined incomes of his children may have approached his earnings.

As a large proportion of the labor force was drawn from the farm sector, in many cases the fertility decision had been made prior to the migration to the mill village. After the move to the mill village, the parents could increase but not decrease the total number of births. White southern families as a group tended to have large numbers of children in comparison with the rest of the United States population, as shown by the data in Table 5-1. When plans for the optimal number and quality of children were formulated early in the marriage, it may be assumed that these households typically expected to continue earning their living upon the land.[10] Unfortunately, many families did not adequately anticipate the precipitous decline in cotton prices from the post-Civil War peak. As a result of the lack of crop diversification and overextension of credit, bankruptcies were numerous.

The labor market environment or location decision was a choice variable for the family. A job search may be conducted within different geographical locales or environments. The payoffs from job search may vary depending on the characteristics of the various labor markets and the current endowments of children. Large families in the southern piedmont farm area perhaps found it particularly advantageous to leave the family farm and migrate to the cotton mill village. A location that offered the prospect of employment for children would be relatively more attractive to a family with many children than to a small family because the incremental gain to family earnings would be larger. Also, the expected maximum job offer for the family as a whole tended to be higher in the mill village than on the farm, providing incentive for migration. Further, there were costs, both real and psychic, associated with migration. If there were a fixed cost of migration, this would tend to screen out the small families. Since the net payoff from migration would be greater for large families, differential migration patterns would be expected.

The decline in agriculture coincided with the boom in the southern textile industry, which offered an alternative occupation. The families who could not earn an adequate

Table 5-1. Average Family Size

	1890	1900
Total U.S. Population	4.93	4.76
South (Whites only)	5.24	5.11
North (Whites only)	4.78	4.65

Number of Children Ever Born per 1000 White Women,
15–49 Years Old

| | | Standardized for | |
	Unstandardized	Age	Age and Marital Status
United States	1884	1995	2026
South	2312	2601	2512
Northeast	1677	1713	1839

Sources: Paul C. Glick, "Family Trends in the United States, 1890–1940" *American Sociological Review* 7 (August 1942): 512; U.S. Bureau of the Census, *Population: Differential Fertility, 1940 and 1910: Fertility By Duration of Marriage* (Washington: Government Printing Office, 1947), pp. 11–12.

income on the farm moved to the mill village. Large farm families may have experienced great difficulty in achieving an adequate income per person on a small plot of land and were thus more likely to transfer to the mill. This effect would be strengthened for families with a relatively high proportion of daughters. Although girls were less highly regarded than boys as hands on the farm, young female spinners commanded higher wages than male doffers. Also a widow with several children would be attracted to the mill as the employment prospects for women and children were more favorable in the mill than on the farm.[11] Therefore, the mill labor force was originally drawn from a population with high fertility; and further, from within this group, the probability of migration was generally highest for those with a large number of children.

Both demand and supply considerations influenced the probability that the unusually large farm families would tend to change occupations and move into the mill village. During the period of labor shortage after 1905, the mills engaged agents who traveled to the remote mountain regions to recruit workers, as discussed in Chapter 1. The agents were commissioned to seek exceptionally large families, reinforcing the trend for the migration of large families. As the mill experienced increasing difficulty in hiring additional workers, an adult male worker who could bring with him other new workers from his family was preferred to a man with no children. In a letter written by a manager of the Alamance Mill on November 19, 1905, it was stated: "I am needing a man to drive wagon. Will pay $5.25 per week. . . . Prefer a man with some hands to work in mill if I can get them."[12] The conditional probability of employment given that the family had a large number of (older) children exceeded the corresponding probability for a small family. From the perspective of supply side considerations, these same large families represented the households who were likely to accept the shift to the manufacturing sector. Labor income of the family was usually increased by mill employment, and the presence of children increased the likelihood of entering this occupation.

The housing arrangements for mill operatives were designed to attract large families with several older children. The size of the house assigned to a family and the number of rooms in it were functions not of household family size per se but rather of the number of workers residing in the home. Children too young to work would only add to the crowding in the house. However, from a life-cycle viewpoint, the youngest children were perceived as the future entrants into the labor force. Housing was not routinely allocated to single-member households. Nonetheless, these individuals were able to secure accommodations as boarders in village homes. The prevalence of boarding arrangements would tend to weaken but not offset the influence of the housing system upon the size of the family unit.

Abstracting from the financial gain to the family from child employment, the costs of rearing a child or providing child care of a given quality would differ between the farm and the mill. Access to educational facilities was greater in the mill village than in sparsely populated farm communities. The mill owners committed substantial resources to the sponsorship of schools and actively encouraged school attendance for the young children. The length of the school term, one indicator of school quality, was typically greater in the mill village than in the mountains. Moreover, many mountain counties lacked schools entirely. Recruiters lauded this advantage of the mill, hoping to entice large families there. The availability of good schools offered further incentive for migration.

Relatively large families initially tended to migrate to the mill village. Further, the employment of mill village children may have provided economic incentive for continued high fertility within the mill community. However, a relatively young marital age among cotton mill workers also may have influenced fertility decisions.

The early marriage of cotton mill workers has been frequently noted by contemporary observers of the southern cotton textile industry.[13] To assess whether cotton mill workers in Alamance County tended to marry at a very early age, we may investigate the age and marital status of 111 cotton mill operatives in Coble Township of Alamance County. The sample drawn from the 1900 Manuscript Census records included 36 Alamance Mill employees. Table 5-2 provides information on the age and conjugal status of the workers between the ages of 10 and 34.

To supplement the information given for each worker, the age and marital status of the additional members of these workers' families or households were also determined. Table 5-3 presents the age and marital status for both the workers and members of their families between the ages of 10 and 34 who were not employed by the mill.

Table 5-2. Marital Status of Cotton Mill Operatives, Coble Township, Alamance County, 1900

Age	Number Single	Number Married	Proportion Married (%)
Males			
10–14	11	0	0
15–19	10	0	0
20–24	6	7	54
25–29	6	13	68
30–34	0	3	100
Females			
10–14	14	0	0
15–19	16	0	0
20–24	8	2	20
25–29	7	1	13
30–34	4	0	0

Source: 1900 Manuscript Census Sample. See Appendix A.

Table 5-3. Marital Status of Cotton Mill Operatives and Additional
Household Members, Coble Township, Alamance County, 1900

Age	Number single	Number married	Proportion Married (%)
Males			
10–14	15	0	0
15–19	15	0	0
20–24	8	7	47
25–29	8	13	62
30–34	0	3	100
Females			
10–14	22	0	0
15–19	18	1	5
20–24	11	10	48
25–29	7	8	53
30–34	4	2	33

Source: 1900 Manuscript Census Sample. See Appendix A.

For an assessment of whether the male workers tended to
marry at an early age, a useful procedure was suggested by
the 1900 Census Report. "The proportion of married men
from 20 to 25 years of age is a good measure of the relative
frequency of early marriages among the native and foreign
white ... elements of the male population."[14] Within this age
group from the sample, 54 percent of the male workers themselves or 47 percent of all males in employee households were
married. As a basis of comparison, according to the Census
Report of 1900, the proportion married among all native white
males of native parentage was only 23.3 percent in the United
States and 29 percent in the state of North Carolina for this
class of population.[15] Therefore, the relatively high proportion
of married males in the 20 to 24 age group found in the sample
offers support to the claim that male cotton mill workers tended
to marry at a relatively young age. This observation may reflect
the derived consequences of selective recruitment of large families as well as conditions of mill village life which tended to
foster early marriage.

In contrast, the group of women within the same sample
do not seem to have married at an unusually young age. For
example, there were no married teenage female mill workers.

Even when the sample was expanded to include both workers
and their households, only 5 percent of the women in the age
group 15 to 19 were married. This statistic compares with 12.2
percent of native white females of native parentage in this age
bracket in the United States or 14 percent for this class in the
state of North Carolina.[16]

Furthermore, we may expand the data set presented in the
above tables to include all individuals between the ages 10 and
55 residing in the homes of textile workers in Coble Township
of Alamance County. The enlarged data set allows us to develop
indirect estimates of the age of marriage. These data provide
the basis for calculation of the "singulate mean age at marriage."
This procedure provides an estimate of the mean age of first
marriage. For the sample group the mean singulate age of marriage is 27.97 for males and 28.4 for females.[17]

Although the data on women in Coble Township are perhaps
at variance with the claim that cotton mill workers tended to
marry at an early age, the data for the men are generally consistent with the industry-wide pattern.

It is interesting to note that among the women in their early
thirties, the women who worked in the mill were all single,
while the women who did not work in the mill were all married.
Although no strong conclusions can be formulated due to the
small sample size and the selectivity bias in the composition of
the sample, the above observation is consistent with the frequently observed pattern that labor force participation rates of
married women are lower than the corresponding rates for single women.

The impact of mill employment may have tended to hasten
the age of marriage. In the farm community, the young adults
may have delayed marriage in order to save for the purchase
of a small plot of land. As both the male and female could
obtain gainful employment with a steady flow of income in the
mill, the pressure to delay marriage was thereby weakened.
Furthermore, if a young couple had grown up in the mill village, they likely had both worked in the mill as soon as they
reached the minimum age of employment. Consequently, they
had already accumulated experience and benefited from on-the-
job training which would be reflected in their wages. The early

labor force participation would thereby accelerate the transition to financial independence for the young adults.

Nevertheless, strong conclusions in comparison with the farm sector are unwarranted. As an alternative to farm ownership, tenancy or share-cropping provided a means of support for a family while the family saved for the eventual purchase of land. During 1880, 21.5 percent of the farms in the Cotton South were operated by white households under tenancy arrangements.[18] Perhaps a wife was considered to be an asset in securing a tenancy arrangement because there would then be at least two workers come harvest time.[19]

If we accept the conclusion that early marriage was a prevalent practice in most southern textile communities, then we must analyze the impact of the marital decision upon fertility choices. There are a few economic dimensions of the marital decision to be analyzed here, including the probability of conception and the parental satisfaction deriving from children while they remained within the original household unit. The influence of early marital age on fertility and the number of children of the cotton mill families is ambiguous.

On the one hand, marriage at an earlier age among females increases the length of time a woman is exposed to the risk of conception. With imperfect fertility control, the greater the duration of the marital relationship, the higher would be fertility, and, all other factors equal, the greater the number of children. It is assumed that illegitimate births constituted only a small fraction of total births in the mill village, due to the strong moral sanctions against premarital sex.

On the other hand, when the interaction and feedback effects between early marriage and child labor are considered, the effect on family size is unclear. The experience gained as a child worker tended to increase the child's later income, facilitating early marriage. Moreover an early marriage, other things equal, would be associated with relatively large completed family size. However, the earlier marriage of children may diminish the satisfaction derived from children, because the children contribute less to the family income stream. The length of time a child remained in the home of the parent may be roughly divided into two periods: when the child was too young to work and the period after the child had entered the mill. An earlier age of marriage diminished the length of time during which the offspring financially contributed to the household, but the initial period of complete financial dependence remained constant. Before the older child left the home, the parents could exert their authority and require the child to seek employment in the mill. A major portion of the child's earnings would then be turned over to the parents. For children over 16 who remained in their parents' home, it has been estimated that the proportions of the child workers' total earnings contributed to the family were 89 percent for females and 72.7 percent for males in 1907.[20] This "property right" in children, the control over their labor services and compensation, would be effectively lost to the parents when the children entered into matrimony.

When the loss of this property right occurred at an earlier age, the benefit of children to parents would correspondingly decline. Thus, a tendency for planned family size to fall with the decrease in total financial contribution from the child might be expected. Alternatively, there might be incentive to expand the family to assure a continued flow of financial resources over the same time horizon. By increasing family size, the parents could continue to exercise their property rights over the newest or youngest members of the family after the older children had married and left home. When the older children married and therefore withdrew from the family labor force, the additional younger children of the family could serve as replacements. As long as some members of the family household continued to work in the mill, the parents could continue residing in the company house after they retired from labor force participation.

There is some evidence available to document the relatively large family size among cotton mill workers. One invaluable study by the Milbank Memorial Fund compared the fertility of 1,353 married women in the mill villages in Greenville, South Carolina, with fertility patterns observed in the poor areas of five northern cities as well as Bushwick, Columbus, Syracuse, and the Lower East Side of New York.[21] Of the Greenville group, the husbands of 24 percent of the wives had been employed in a different occupation when they were first married. This suggests the proportion of families drawn from the farm sector to the mill community. The fertility data are

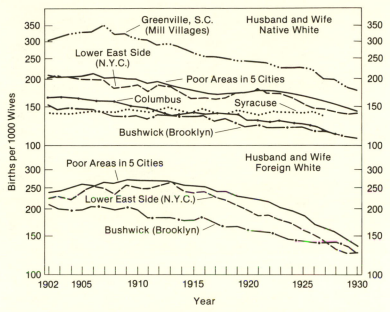

Figure 5-1. Milbank Memorial Fund Fertility Study. Areal differences in levels and trends of birth rates among native and foreign white married women of childbearing age. Standardized annual rates per 1000 married women under 45 years of age are five-year moving averages. Source: Clyde V. Kiser, "Trends in Annual Birth Rates Among Married Women in Selected Areas According to Nativity, Age, and Social Class," *Milbank Memorial Fund Quarterly Bulletin* 15 (January 1937):54.

based on retrospective family history data and therefore may reflect selective migration effects. The highest birthrate among native women in the study was recorded in the textile community of Greenville, as indicated by Figures 5-1 and 5-2 reproduced from that study.

From data collected in another important study, family size in a major textile state in New England may be compared with a major textile state in the South. The U.S. Commissioner of Labor surveyed families in 1891 headed by fathers who worked in cotton textile mills.[22] From the data, average family size could be calculated for the cotton manufacturing states of Massachusetts and North Carolina. Table 5-4 reports both the average family size in the two textile centers as well as the family

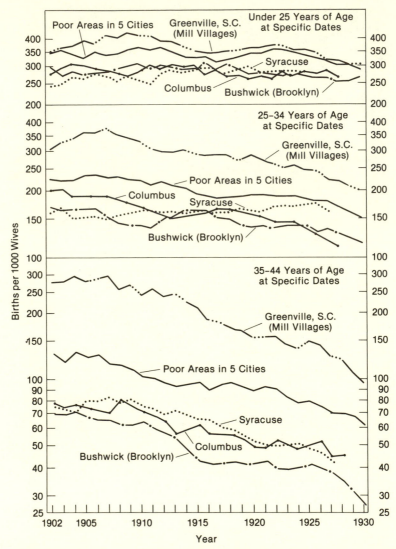

Figure 5-2. Milbank Memorial Fund Fertility Study. Areal comparisons in levels and trends of birth rates among native white married women of specific ages. Source: Clyde V. Kiser, "Trends in Annual Birth Rates Among Married Women in Selected Areas According to Nativity, Age, and Social Class," *Milbank Memorial Fund Quarterly Bulletin* 15 (January 1937):60.

Table 5-4. Family Size in 1891 Among Families in Which Male, Native-born, Head-of-Household Worked in a Cotton Textile Mill

Family Size	North Carolina	Massachusetts
Average family size	5.74	4.61
Number of cases	95	143

Family Size Distribution: Number of Family Members	Percentage of Families with Given Family Size North Carolina	 Massachusetts
2–3	18	32
4–5	34	38
6–7	28	24
8–9	17	6
10–11	5	—

Source: U.S. Commissioner of Labor, Seventh Annual Report, *Cost of Production: The Textiles and Glass*, vol. 2, part 2, "Cost of Living," House Document #2958, 52nd Congress, 2d. Sess. (Washington, D.C.: Government Printing Office): 876–877, 877–889.

size distributions in each state. The data, which are not standardized by age at marriage, are based upon the number of surviving children in the home. As expected, in North Carolina, where the practice of child labor was more extensive than in New England and where many workers brought to the mill high fertility mores of the farm, families were larger than in Massachusetts.

For the same year, 1891, data on 46 North Carolina mill families were collected by the North Carolina Bureau of Labor Statistics. The average family size among this survey group was 5.3 members.[23]

The records of the Alamance Mill provide additional information on family size. Seventeen Alamance Mill families were identified by comparing the payroll records with the 1900 Manuscript Census reports. From this group, two to eight immediate family members resided in the home in 1900, with an average size of 5.5 members. As a basis of comparison, in 1900 the modal family size in the United States was 4 persons, and the mean family size was 4.76.[24]

During 1907, 854 New England mill families and 1,567 southern mill families were surveyed in a Senate investigative study. The average size of families, in which the head of household was native-born and of native parentage, was 5.5 members in New England and 6.6 members in the South.[25] Again, the number of family members in the home was larger in the South where child labor was more prevalent and family size was traditionally larger. The average number of wage-earners per household was 2.9 in New England and 3.8 in the South.

An analysis of the nonpecuniary satisfaction derived from children is usually considered beyond the sphere of economic analysis. Children represented a source of happiness apart from their earnings. Perhaps, due to the mores of the society or religious beliefs, a couple married for a long time with no children felt somewhat disgraced for having failed to fulfill their social obligation. Nevertheless, the pro-natal morality was undoubtedly fostered, to some extent, by the economic interests within a community where the practice of child labor was common.[26] During 1883 a pamphlet written in North Carolina proclaimed, "Nature intended every man to be the father of four or five children, at least." To do otherwise was to "violate one of the fundamental rules of natural law and, thereby, incur the wrath of God, deprive himself of happiness, and his State of citizens."[27]

Alternatively, childbearing may have been viewed with hopeless resignation; children were perhaps thought to be the byproduct of marriage, particularly in light of the generally limited information regarding contraceptive methods. Contraceptive information was probably less widely disseminated, for both black and white groups, in the South than in the rest of the nation. In their study of the lower social class of the South which included the mill workers, during the period from 1911 to 1941, Allison Davis, Burleigh Gardner, and Mary Gardner concluded that children were regarded simply as

> an inevitable result of sexual relations. Married couples expect to have children; and, as far as can be ascertained, they make little effort to prevent conception. Contraceptive methods are little known and little used. Apparently, continence is the general method of birth control when any control is considered, as in the case of a young wife, who having had five children in four years, said that she and her husband had ceased sexual relations in order to avoid having more children.[28]

Rupert Vance expressed his perception of the general attitude toward contraceptive behavior: "Here we are concerned with groups on whom the ordinary prudential controls weigh so lightly that such means are but little used."[29]

Demographic characteristics of the southern population usually associated with high fertility include the high rural proportion and the relatively young age of the population. In a study analyzing the high fertility of the South in 1930, Vance concluded that a locational fertility differential remained, even after correcting for the age composition and rural setting:

> Over half of the area's extra fertility is simply due to the tendency of women in the region—irrespective of race, rurality, or of age difference—to have more children. Given the race, the rural-urban, and the age distribution characteristic of the Nation, births in the Southeast would be reduced only 6.2 percent. This higher specific fertility may be taken as an index of the lag in the practice of family limitation in the region.[30]

Although Robert Willis has assumed in his model that fertility control was costless, perhaps the actual cost of control was prohibitive or the wherewithal to limit fertility was unavailable. Alternatively, the economic environment may not have provided incentive to practice family limitation.

In conclusion, the southern piedmont cotton textile industry labor force was drawn primarily from the farm sector where families tended to be large. Children were a source of both direct satisfaction to their parents as well as indirect satisfaction deriving from their gainful employment. Mill managers structured the labor recruitment policies so as to induce the selective migration of relatively large farm families to the mill villages. Moreover, the economic environment of the cotton mill village was conducive to the continuation of high fertility patterns. The family labor system, mill paternalism, and pro-natal social climate reinforced the perception of the desirability of a large family. Therefore, there may have been strong economic motivation for both the rural farm families from which the labor supply was drawn and for the current mill village dwellers to choose not to practice family limitation.

This chapter has analyzed the impact of the family labor system upon the family unit itself. In order to provide a richer treatment of the labor supply process, the following chapter explores the conditions conducive to the original adoption of the family labor system.

6

Conclusions

The southern cotton textile industry during the postbellum period was able to mobilize the labor services of workers transferred from the agricultural community. The preceding chapters have established the internal logic of the patterns of labor deployment adopted in order to secure a disciplined factory workforce. These chapters have analyzed the interaction and adaptation between the mills and the workers, the difficulties confronting the mills in recruiting and training a corps of workers, and the dramatic alteration in the social and economic lives of the mill families as the household farm was replaced by the mill village as the place of residence and work environment.

Several broad questions arise concerning the rationale for the emergence of the system of labor organized on the basis of the family unit. Why did southern mills adopt the family labor system rather than some other system of labor organization? Alternatively, a broader question may be posed: What are the general conditions conducive to the adoption of a family labor system? Finally, one must also consider the scope or range of options available to southern cotton textile managers in the selection of a pattern of labor deployment. How fluid or determined were the social and economic structures?

A comparison of alternative labor arrangements in the textile industry provides invaluable insight into the unique conditions fostering the development of a family labor system. Therefore, the experiences of the Lowell cotton mills in Massachusetts before 1850 and the Japanese cotton mills after 1890 are contrasted with the southern case. In both the Lowell mills and the Japanese mills the workforce was composed mostly of single females housed in company operated or supervised dormitories.

The workforce at the Lowell mills was composed predominantly of unmarried women living near the mills in boarding houses. Thomas Dublin has carefully investigated the composition of a large sample group of employees from the Hamilton Mills during 1836. At that time 85 percent of the workers on the payroll of this representative mill were female. Males were employed as supervisors and mechanics. The labor pool was relatively homogeneous in age and nationality as well; most workers were women in their late teens and twenties who had been born and raised in New England. Less than 4 percent of the workers were foreign-born, and 80 percent of the women over 10 years of age were between the ages of 15 and 30. Children were conspicuously absent in comparison with the South, as only 3 percent of the workers were younger than 15 years of age.[1]

The Japanese mills relied even more heavily upon the labor services of single females than the early New England mills. The proportion of females reached unprecedented levels as evidenced by Table 6-1. During the 1890s, the average age among female workers was only 19. A much higher proportion of children worked in the Japanese mills than in Lowell.

Table 6-1. Females as a Percentage of the Cotton Textile Labor Force

Year	Japan	Year	United States	Year	United Kingdom	Year	India
1909	83.0	1830	66.0	1835	55.1	1884	22.5
1914	83.3	1850	63.0	1847	58.7	1894	25.9
1920	80.0	1890	54.5	1867	61.3	1909	22.1
1925	80.6	1910	48.3	1878	62.7	1924	21.6
1930	80.6	1919	42.4	1895	62.3	1934	18.9

Source: Gary R. Saxonhouse, "Country Girls and Communication Among Competitors in the Japanese Cotton-Spinning Industry," in *Japanese Industrialization and Its Social Consequences,* ed. by Hugh Patrick (Berkeley: University of California Press, 1976), p. 100.

Approximately 30 percent of the Japanese workers were age 14 or younger.[2] The female workers were communally housed in dormitories.

In all three cases of textile development, workers were induced to migrate from the agrarian sector to the manufacturing sector. An examination of the financial state of the family farm helps us understand the emergence of different patterns of labor organization and workforce composition. The economic viability of the family farm would strongly determine or influence the supply price of labor, as farming represented the major alternative occupation. Furthermore, whether the children in a household would later be able to own sufficient land must also be assessed. Even if the farm were currently profitable, would aspirations by the children for continuing in the traditional family occupation of independent farming go unfulfilled?

Farming in New England in the early nineteenth century represented a viable means of earning a livelihood. Nonetheless, opportunities within the agricultural sector were stagnating. The western regions of the United States achieved a comparative advantage in the production of foodstuffs for the market, leading to a relative decline in the earnings on the New England farm. Much of the land in New England was rocky or marginal. Nevertheless, as long as the farm continued to be profitable, despite the increasingly gloomy prospects, the head-of-household tended to remain in his traditional occupation on the farm. The response to the closing of opportunities for entry into the occupation of independent farming and the ownership of land came not from the head-of-household but from the older, mature offspring. Alexander Field states that "It was primarily those entering the labor force for the first time who made the relevant decisions."[3] Some young workers, particularly males, migrated westward. Many of the young females who remained in New England made their way into the factories.

The Lowell women then came from farms experiencing some financial distress but certainly not financial ruin. Dublin surveyed a group of fathers of female mill workers from New Hampshire. He observed that 86 percent of the parents in the sample held property valued at $100 or more. The families of the mill women represented the "broad middle ranges of wealth." He therefore concludes that the economic needs of the family did not provide a compelling force in the decision for the women to enter the mill, a view shared by Caroline Ware.[4] A personnel agent engaged by a Lowell mill believed that "their sole object in leaving home and coming here from places so remote, and entering upon an entirely new course of life, is to make more money by their exertions than they can in any other employment."[5] The alternative occupations available to females such as domestic service were limited and generally offered lower compensation.

The continuing viability of the Japanese household farm also conditioned the transfer of females rather than males or whole families to the cotton mills. The value of the labor of male heads of household substantially exceeded that of other family members, particularly the girls. If a father were to relocate to the factory setting, he would take his family with him. According to Yukio Masui, the cost of labor outflow on a family basis was found to be greater than that for individuals due to costs associated with closing out the farm entirely and the cost of severing ties with the rural village.[6] Furthermore, job security for all family members was lower and opportunities for housewives and the aged were more limited in the non-farm sector. In contrast, the value of the daughter to the farm sector simply equaled the wage earnings of a female farm laborer.

The argument developed by Masui supports the selection of a system of labor organization directed toward the individual, rather than a family. The research of Robert Cole and Ken'ichi Tominaga provides a complementary explanation of the decision to hire the young daughters rather than the sons of farm families on an individual basis. Despite the relatively small acreage per worker in Japan, the cultivation of rice was labor intensive. Significant labor-saving innovations were not implemented in rice production until after World War II. "Therefore, agricultural households could not afford to allow their workforce, other than unmarried females, to flow out of the villages." The daughters were not considered part of the permanent workforce of the family farm as it was expected that they would eventually marry and move away to live with their husbands. In contrast, the expectation that the male children would remain in agriculture was deeply rooted. With regard to the sons, "Agriculture was perceived in terms of a livelihood (*nariwai*), that is, as life itself."[7] These cultural bonds to the farm were particularly strong for the eldest son, who would eventually inherit the family farm.

In sharp contrast to the state of farming in New England and Japan, it is recalled from earlier chapters that the southern workers in the late nineteenth century were recruited from a poverty-stricken farm sector. Families were faced with financial ruin as the household farms were lost to bankruptcy. Tenancy arrangements often afforded only minimal subsistence. Even as farm prospects began to improve, expected family income was generally higher in the mill village than on the tenant farm. Due to the impoverished conditions in the farm sector, the value of the labor of adult males would have been relatively low in the South. Therefore, just as the existence of profitable or feasible alternatives in farming in New England or Japan tended to make male wages in those factories prohibitively expensive, the lack thereof in the South contributed to the relative cheapness of adult male labor in the southern mills. Then, given the decision to attract mature adult males to the mill, there was further incentive for management to hire additional family members as well. As discussed in the previous chapters, the cost of employing additional family members was relatively low as long as total family income was high enough to attract the household unit to the mill village. Further, the South lacked a well-developed female agricultural wage labor market. Family employment in the mill offered a parent some of the benefits of "property rights" in his children that he might have hoped for as a farm owner.

Claudia Goldin and Kenneth Sokoloff have further analyzed the differential pattern of industrial development between the Northeast and the South. They offer an important explanation of the differential utilization of women and children between the two regions. They attribute the regional variation largely to significant differences in the relative value of labor. Southern agriculture was characterized by high relative productivity, and hence high relative wages, of women and children. "Thus, females and children, although employed by cotton textiles in the South, formed a smaller percentage of its labor force than they had done in the North earlier in the century."[8]

The "relative productivity hypothesis" suggests a complementary explanation for the selection of the family labor system in the South. At any given level of output, southern mill managers would tend to employ a higher ratio of adult males to women and children. Perhaps southern managers would have encountered community opposition had they attempted to obtain the optimal distribution of workers by hiring individuals rather than family units. In the Lowell mills, most of the women were young and single. However, given the social mores of the South, perhaps reliance upon single women in the factory alongside adult men was difficult or unacceptable. As one mill manager stated, "we prefer families of daughters presided over by a good father to promiscuous girls boarding." He further stressed that "We have but two unmarried men in our mill and these do not board with girls."[9]

Although management sponsored paternalistic activities in all three of the industrial settings, perhaps paternalism was more effective in stabilizing and improving the quality of workers when workers were recruited as family units rather than on an individual basis. The economic motivation for the provision of comprehensive welfare activities in the southern mill village has been extensively discussed in previous chapters. In contrast, Gary Saxonhouse has determined that the welfare programs instituted by the Japanese mills were ineffective in promoting worker stability. Despite the commitment of substantial resources to paternalistic endeavors, he found that the average tenure of an entering worker did not increase. He further suggested that "a bundle of job characteristics weighted with nonpecuniary benefits was [not] necessarily an efficient means of attracting workers."[10]

The wage structure in Japan fostered the transient nature of work and high turnover rates. In order to attract new workers, recruiting agents were employed to entice families to send their daughters into the mills. As an effective method of persuasion, the mills advanced a substantial bonus payment to the parent, equivalent to the earnings for twenty days of work, in return for a contractual commitment for the labor services of the daughter. However, as the starting daily wage was lower than the alternative farm wage, there was incentive for the girls to run away from the mill and secure employment elsewhere. The wages of workers with more than two years' experience exceeded the farm labor wage; however, it was costly and difficult for the workers to finance the initial period of training. Hence, turnover was high. During 1897 a survey of 75 mills revealed that more than 40 percent of first-time workers left the mill within six months, and fewer than 5 percent of the cotton textile workers had more than five years' experience.[11]

Paternalism did not contribute to the development of a workforce permanently attached to the Japanese mills. From every cohort of new workers, a few workers would stay on and gradually increase the pool of experienced workers. Saxonhouse concluded that the increase in average experience was attributable to this effect only, with no change in individual persistence rates.[12] Given the striking degree of uniformity in technique among the Japanese mills, skills acquired through on-the-job training programs were easily transferable. Since trained workers could easily transfer to another mill, mill managers acted to keep the costs of training to a minimum. Therefore, the wage structure was designed to shift the cost of training to the worker, even though this contributed to the instability of the workforce.

In contrast, the family labor system in the South effectively limited individual mobility, enhancing the specific qualities of a training program and lowering turnover rates. The mill managers therefore were willing to offer on-the-job training as well as basic education in mill schools. If the mill were successful in retaining a mature adult operative for a period of time, the other family members stayed on as well. A child who was raised in the mill village and who had entered the mill at a young age then had incentive to remain as a mill worker during adulthood. In the case of the Alamance Mill, mobility was further diminished by the ownership of the majority of the surrounding mills by the Holt family. With effective limitations on mobility, the mills would thereby be able to recoup the costs of schooling and training over a longer period of time.

Tamara Hareven has emphasized the importance of studying the family life cycle in order to understand the dynamic response of the family to industrialization.[13] In the South, a large family's hopes of maintaining an adequate standard of living on the traditional family farm began to fade away as cotton prices remained low. Compelled by economic necessity, the southern parents decided to relocate their families to the cotton mill village. Typically neither the parents nor the children returned to the agricultural sector. As the older children tended to marry within the mill community, Herbert Lahne wrote that "cotton mill work becomes almost a hereditary occupation."[14]

In New England, the entry of daughters into the factory involved the geographical and occupational separation of the nuclear family, whereas in the South the pattern of labor organization preserved family cohesion. When the older children of the New England farm families entered the labor force, women found more lucrative opportunities in the cotton textile industry than in their parents' traditional occupation. Personnel agents toured the countryside of Vermont, New Hampshire, Maine, and Massachusetts, recruiting young women to work in the Lowell mills. Nevertheless, ties to the family were not abruptly severed, as communication was maintained through regular visits and letters. Gradually the mill was assured of a steady stream of job applicants who were informed of potential openings by friends and relatives of those currently employed in the mill. The development of a network of familial and friendship bonds among the workers was associated with an increase in tenure among workers. Preferential treatment in job assignment was accorded to workers recruited in this manner, and the average duration of employment for employees who worked with relatives was 3.7 years, while the corresponding tenure for workers with no relatives in the mill was only 2.2 years.[15] The development of the broader kin network had a stabilizing influence on the workforce, although the effect was undoubtedly somewhat weaker than when the nuclear family as a unit transferred to the mill setting.

The women who entered the Lowell mills tended to marry at a later age than their counterparts who remained in the farm sector. However, after marriage, by custom, women rarely returned to work in the mills. From a sample of 45 mill workers who eventually married, Dublin found that although two-thirds of the women had come from farm families, less than one-third of the women married farmers. Dublin commented, "For many, work in Lowell proved to be a first, and an irreversible, step away from the rural, agricultural lives of their parents. . . . The world of their parents was the world of their past; they had moved beyond."[16]

Also in Japan, the work experience in the mill represented only a brief, transitory phase in the life cycle of a woman between leaving her parents' farm and entering into matrimony. Unlike the female workers in Lowell, however, the Japanese girls usually returned to the rural village to marry farmers.

Then, according to custom, the woman was expected to remain in the home, with the husband financially responsible for the family.[17]

A final dimension of the family labor system that remains to be investigated is the scope or degree of freedom that existed for directing the outcome of the labor supply process and the development of a disciplined workforce. Morris Morris perceives that management can narrowly determine the path of development of the labor supply process. From his study of the emergence of an industrial workforce in India, Morris concluded that management was generally able to select and effectively implement the desired pattern of labor organization, supporting the position that management may dictate the direction of the labor supply process. Morris maintains that "the basic quality of labor performance as it emerged in the cotton textile industry [in India] was the result of employer policy and responses to market forces and not the consequence of labor force psychology or social structure." Further, "there is no question that early employers were free to choose virtually any pattern of work organization they desired."[18]

Herbert Lahne, in his treatment of the southern mill experience, adopted a relatively narrow approach to labor history. His basic concern was the failure of the movement to organize labor unions in the southern cotton textile industry. He attributed this outcome almost entirely to the deliberate strategies developed by management in opposition to the workers. In this respect, his writing is similar to the research of Morris. According to Lahne, paternalism represented the means to assure compliance with management's plans for labor mobilization. Moreover, the dependence fostered by the paternalistic relationship provided the justification for the continuation of the welfare system. The worker found himself in a situation in which "every aspect of his life [was] subject to manipulation by the employer."[19] Hence, the mill managers were able to prevent the development of worker consciousness.

Recent research in the history of the family has stressed the importance of relating the analysis of the family to the structure and institutions of the society within an interdisciplinary framework. Similarly, the field of inquiry for research in labor history has also been broadened to take into account the influence of the cultural milieu upon the labor supply process. Recent historical research highlights the significant constraints or limitations on management's sphere of control imposed by the cultural environment. The works of E. P. Thompson, Herbert Gutman, Joan Scott, and Louise Tilly place major emphasis upon the power or influence exerted by the customs, the values, and the social institutions in shaping the outcome of the labor supply process.[20]

Wilbur Cash, in his exploration of the unique character of the southern individual, examines the ways in which the deeply rooted cultural heritage played a crucial role in the formation of patterns of labor deployment.[21] Although movement to the cotton mill dramatically altered the worker's way of life, the system of labor organization was dominated nonetheless by a basic historical continuity of traditional social relations and institutions. The mill village was perceived to be an extension of the pre-Civil War plantation system of labor organization. The establishment of the plantation system in the factory setting provided a social justification for the domination of the factory workers by the factory managers. Therefore, although Cash perceived that the boundaries of management's capacity to control or mold the labor supply process were limited by the existing social structure and traditions, these same cultural foundations provided the basis of strength for management to control the workers.

Certainly the tradition of a paternalistic society was founded in the Old South. According to Eugene Genovese, paternalism in the antebellum South, which tended to align the individual worker with management, "grew out of the necessity to discipline and morally justify a system of exploitation."[22] Nevertheless, as Genovese reminds us, a whole group of people, such as the black slaves or the postbellum cotton mill operatives, retain the ability to exert some degree of control over their environment.

This book has analyzed the labor process whereby a growing industry was able to attract and develop a labor force recruited from the farm sector. The interaction between the mill and the families represented a resolution of the tensions or challenges introduced by the shift from the household farm to the mill village and factory setting. The character of the available labor supply fostered the adoption of the family labor system, and the outcome of the labor supply process was the result of the complex interrelationship between the mill and the workers. The southern cotton mill village was neither a world wholly created by the mill managers nor was it solely a community created by the cotton mill operatives.

Epilogue

The mill village or company town was a hallmark of the postbellum southern cotton textile industry. Commencing in the 1930s and accelerating after World War II, the textile firms began selling off their company-owned housing. The dissolution of this important institution represented a major break from tradition. The reversal of the long established customary policy of providing subsidized housing in the mill village reflected the changing industrial relations within the industry.

During the postbellum period many workers migrated from farms to the mill villages. The family labor system and mill paternalism were adopted as a response to the novice factory labor force. The terms of employment were initially designed to promote stability, training, and discipline of the workforce. Over time the state of the labor market gradually changed. As the industry evolved, the composition of the labor force was transformed, and new styles of management were implemented. Thus, the traditional mill village had outgrown its usefulness, and the company-town environment no longer served the best interests of the firm.

Under the family labor system, several members of a family were hired to work together in the mill. With the passage of time, the number of workers per family tended to decline. Therefore, a family occupying a company-owned house supplied fewer workers to the factory, increasing the cost per worker of the rent subsidy. Child labor, an integral component of the family labor system, had largely disappeared as a result of changes in supply and demand. Labor force participation rates of young workers declined substantially as family incomes increased. Furthermore, with the enactment of the federally mandated minimum wage, the cost of employing young workers became prohibitive. The labor productivity of the young workers was generally too low to justify their continued employment at the new higher wage levels.

During the years of rapid growth in the industry, new workers were continually recruited to fill the ranks of mill operatives. Mill employees were assured that jobs would be made available for their children when they were old enough to join the labor force. This practice helped serve an important recruiting function by economizing on hiring costs. Older members of the family would assist in training and supervising the younger workers. By hiring family groups, the firms may have traded away some flexibility in the selection of individual workers but were thereby reducing turnover and monitoring costs. As the decades passed, the balance of the benefits and costs tilted, reducing the interest of management in retaining the mill village system. Vacancies were increasingly filled by experienced factory workers in the region rather than from novice workers recently transferred from the farm sector. Growth in the industry slowed. The provision of housing was no longer deemed necessary for recruitment. Many mills were located in more densely populated regions, and transportation improvements allowed workers to live at greater distances from the factory. After World War II, racial barriers began to lift, further expanding the potential pool of job applicants.

With the introduction of industrial engineering and techniques of scientific management, managerial efficiency replaced the paternalistic style of the early mill owners. Whereas previously workers were assured direct access to owners and top management, professional personnel officers assumed a more detached, impersonal style of management. Oftentimes owners were absent altogether. Moreover, opposition by workers to the comprehensive welfare programs intensified during the first half of the twentieth century. Prompted by the drive to reduce costs and increase efficiency, managers significantly reduced the scope of company-sponsored welfare activities. The sale of company-owned housing tended to lower fixed overhead costs of the firm. Moreover, local public school districts assumed greater responsibility for improving the quality of education, decreasing the importance of maintaining separate mill village schools.

As reliance on the family labor system diminished, the strength of mill paternalism waned. The terms of employment were gradually restructured toward individual workers, rather than whole families. Hence, the mill village sales symbolized the disappearance of the family labor system in the southern cotton textile industry.

Appendix A

Description and Preparation of the
Alamance Mill Data Set

This appendix provides a description of the primary data sets for the Alamance Mill and Alamance County, North Carolina. Heavy reliance has been placed upon the comprehensive company records of the Alamance Mill. The voluminous mill records include the daily payroll books from 1890 to 1912, the business correspondence file, output records, inventory and shipping books, invoices, bank accounts, the rental housing ledger from 1908 to 1920, the company store accounts, and personal diaries. The repository for these invaluable records is the Southern Historical Collection of the University of North Carolina Library in Chapel Hill. In addition, an important supplementary primary data source was the manuscript population census records for Alamance County in 1900 and 1910.

The payroll or time books of the Alamance Mill offered a virtually complete employment record for a 23-year period. During this time period, 271 individuals were employed fulltime for varying lengths of time. The yearly workforce ranged from 52 to 76 workers as indicated by Table A-1.

Daily earnings were based either upon a flat day rate or a piece rate. The weavers, who were generally compensated on a uniform piece-rate basis, differed in their productivity and hence daily earnings. Occupations such as spooler or slubber

Table A-1. Alamance Mill Workforce

Year	No. of Employees	Year	No. of Employees
1890	76	1902	52
1891	66	1903	73
1892	62	1904	67
1893	59	1905	67
1894	65	1906	63
1895	69	1907	61
1896	58	1908	62
1897	63	1909	62
1898	53	1910	60
1899	55	1911	59
1900	57	1912	65
1901	56		

were compensated at a flat daily rate. Because of the huge quantity of individual daily payroll entries, sampling was necessary. The individual weekly earnings data for this study were calculated as the average full-time weekly earnings for an eight-week period during each year. For a worker paid on the basis for a fixed daily rate, it could be readily determined when less than a full day had been worked. However, for a piece-rate worker, only the total output and earnings were recorded with no indication of the number of hours worked. Occasionally a weaver may have worked only three-quarters of the day, but this unfortunately could not be determined from the payroll records.

The daily payroll records yielded information about experience, turnover, and absenteeism among the Alamance Mill workers. For a cohort of workers initially entering the mill after 1890, the length of tenure for subsequent years could be easily determined. The experience variable was measured in half-year units. As the payroll records before 1890 were unavailable, the experience composition of the group of workers employed during 1890 could not always be directly determined. Gavin Wright has developed estimates of the experience levels of the 1890 workforce based on the overall age-experience profile of the 1900 workforce. His estimates have been employed in this study with minor modifications. The estimates were first analyzed for reasonableness. Further information about the data of entry for many individuals could be gleaned from the census reports as well as diaries of mill officials.

Wright assumed that the starting age for workers in 1890 was 16. (The median age of workers who entered the mill after 1890 and whose names were matched with the manuscript census records was 16.) For example, Wright estimated that a sister and her brother had each accumulated eleven years of experience by 1890; the manuscript population census records for 1880 confirm that both workers had been employed in a cotton mill in 1880. Further, the average experience level exhibits an upward trend over time. In order to determine that this pattern was not simply the result of the estimation procedure, the turnover of the cohort group initially entering the mill in 1891 was compared with that of the 1905 group. A worker commencing work in 1891 tended to remain 2.25 years on average, but the average length of employment for a new recruit in 1905 was 3.7 years, suggesting an increase in persistence rates.

The diary of Henderson Monroe Fowler, a mill manager, provided additional information about the tenure of workers. For example, the diary entry of May 30, 1887, reported that "Jerry Boggs [a mill employee] moved to Alamance factory."

The experience variable measures experience accrued within the Alamance Mill. Although on-the-job training in another cotton mill would likely augment productivity in the Alamance Mill, the data on prior work histories were unavailable and were therefore excluded from consideration. A further measurement problem arises due to the possible depreciation of skills when an employee was temporarily out of the labor force. The variable experience was measured as number of years employed in the mill with no adjustment for the discontinuous employment record of certain individuals. For example, one female employee worked in 1905, 1907, 1908, and 1910, and another female worked continuously from 1907 through 1910. In both cases, the recorded experience measured at the end of 1910 was four years.

Further information about the 1900 and 1910 mill families was obtained by matching the names on the payroll records with the manuscript population census rolls for Coble Township in Alamance County. Age, literacy, occupation, and marital status could thereby be determined for this group of 44 workers in

1900 and 49 workers in 1910. Also, the identity of additional family members residing in the home was obtained.

The data set drawn from the 1900 manuscript population census records was expanded to include a total of 348 cotton textile workers and their families in Alamance County. This supplementary sample was jointly prepared by Gavin Wright and this investigator.

Appendix B

Fertility Choice Model That Incorporates Child Labor Income

The following basic fertility choice model assumes that the only satisfaction derived from having children is due to the net financial contribution of the children to the family (earnings of children minus expenditures on children). Admittedly, this assumption represents a serious abstraction from reality. Nevertheless, there is heuristic value to the model. The family is trying to maximize the net income of the family (Y). The wife's working time (l) is divided between market work and child care in the home for a wage.

$$\max Y = H + W_w l_w^m + n W_c \alpha l_c - ns \qquad (1)$$
$$l = l_w^m + l_w^c$$

Y = net income
H = father's earning
W_w = wife's wage
l = wife's working time
l_w^m = wife's time spent in market work
l_w^c = wife's time spent in child care functions
n = number of children
W_c = children's wage rate
αl_c = children's time spent in market work
s = resources or market goods devoted to raising a child, with the normalized price of $s = 1$

The maximization problem may be rewritten as a Lagrangian expression,

$$L = H + W_w l_w^m + nf(l_w^c/n, s)\alpha l_c - ns - \lambda(l_w^m + l_w^c - 1) \quad (2)$$

max W.R.T. n, s, l_w^c, l_w^m; $W_c = f(l_w^c/n, s)$

The function $W_c = f(l_w^c/n, s)$ represents the dependence of the wage of children on factors determining child quality including the amount of time the mother allocated per child in child care activities and market resources devoted to a child, such that

$$\partial f/\partial(l_w^c/n) > 0; \quad \partial^2 f/\partial(l_w^c/n)^2 < 0$$

without some minimum time devoted to the children by the mother, the child would perhaps suffer from malnutrition or lack of basic socialization skills and therefore job productivity would be low. However, after some initial range, the function may have flattened out beyond this minimum time per child, with the second partial derivative becoming "very negative." Also, there may have been scale economies in the provision of the basic minimal care for several children simultaneously. Similarly, $\partial f/\partial s > 0$ and $\partial^2 f/\partial s^2 < 0$.

The first-order conditions that obtain from the maximization are present in equations 3 and 6:

$$\partial L/\partial n = f\alpha l_c - \alpha l_c(l_w^c/n)[\partial f/\partial(l_w^c/n)] - s = 0 \quad (3)$$

$$\partial L/\partial s = n\alpha l_c(\partial f/\partial s) - n = 0 \quad (4)$$

$$\partial L/\partial l_w^c = \alpha l_c[\partial f/\partial(l_w^c/n)] - \lambda = 0 \quad (5)$$

$$\partial L/\partial l_w^m = W_w - \lambda = 0 \quad (6)$$

The optimal number of children is derived from equation 3. Equation 3 may be rewritten as

$$f\alpha l_c = \alpha l_c(l_w^c/n)[\partial f/\partial(l_w^c/n)] + s \quad (7)$$

Accordingly, the number of children should be increased until the additional earnings of the last child equals the cost of rearing another child, where the cost $= s +$ the decrease in child earnings arising from the lower average wage. As the number of children increases, the wife's time per child declines if the wife's time in child care functions remains constant. With less time devoted to a child, quality falls, and hence the child's wage rate declines.

From equation 4,

$$(\partial f / \partial s) \, \alpha l_c = 1 \qquad (8)$$

With more market resources devoted to raising a child, child quality, and hence the wage paid children, both increase. As s increases, total child earnings increase, but the total expenditures for raising the children will also increase. At the margin, the price of market resources will just equal the increase in total earnings by the children as s is increased by one unit.

From equations 5 and 6,

$$\alpha l_c [\partial f / \partial (l_w^c / n)] - \lambda = W_w - \lambda \qquad (9)$$

$$W_w = [\partial f / \partial (l_w^c / n] \, \alpha l_c \qquad (10)$$

The wife devotes time to the children just until the value of their additional earnings equals what she herself could earn in the marketplace.

The above model may be modified by substituting the expected per child earnings for the market wage rate of children, where $E(W_c) = (W_c \times$ probability of employment). This modification recognizes the existence of labor market imperfections, in particular, the rationing of jobs by mill employers in search of a particular type of labor force. If the probability of employment was a positive function of the number of children (or potential workers) in the family as the discussion in Chapter 5 suggests, then it is possible that the family was subject to a form of "increasing returns" to the number of children. In the original formulation of the model, the level of the individual child's wage was a function of the amount of time that the mother was able to allocate per child. However, when the expected per child earnings is considered rather than the wage rate of children, there would perhaps be some increasing returns to scale in the total amount of the mother's time spent in child rearing. If firms preferred large families, then the presence of an additional child may have increased the probability that a sibling would obtain employment.

If the probability of family employment is $p(n)$, where $\partial p / \partial n > 0$ and $\partial^2 p / \partial n^2 < 0$, then the Lagrangian expression for the modified version of the model is

$$L = H + W_w l_w^m + n f(l_w^c / n, s) \, p(n) \, \alpha l_c - ns - \lambda(l_w^m + l_w^c - 1) \qquad (11)$$

The first-order condition for the modified model which corresponds to equation 3 is presented in equation 12:

$$\partial L / \partial n = f(l_w^c / n, s) \, p(n) \, \alpha l_c \qquad (12)$$

$$- [\partial f / \partial (l_w^c / n)](l_w^c / n) \, \alpha l_c \, p(n)$$

$$+ \alpha l_c \, n f(l_w^c / n, s) \, \partial p / \partial n - s = 0$$

Corresponding to equation 7, the above first-order condition may be rewritten as

$$f(l_w^c / n, s) \, p(n) \, \alpha l_c + \alpha l_c n f(l_w^c / n, s) \, \partial p / \partial n \qquad (13)$$

$$= [\partial f / \partial (l_w^c / n)](l_w^c / n) \, \alpha l_c \, p(n) + s$$

To assess the effect of substituting the expected wage of children for the children's wage level, consider two cases. In the first case, assume the probability of employment in the original model equals a constant term $p(n) = \bar{p}$. This yields the following first-order condition:

$$f(l_w^c / n, s) \, \bar{p} \, \alpha l_c = [\partial f / \partial (l_w^c / n)](l_w^c / n) \, \alpha l_c \, p(n) + s \qquad (14)$$

This is equation 7 with $\bar{p}$ in place of W_c; equation 7 implicitly sets $\bar{p} = 1$. With reference to equations 13 and 14, consider how the equilibrium will change when, in the second case, the probability of employment equals $p(n)$ rather than $\bar{p}$. In both cases, the first-order conditions imply that the number of children should be increased until the marginal benefit of an additional child (the left-hand expressions) equals the marginal cost of increasing the number of children (the right-hand expressions). The marginal benefit of children is increased and the marginal cost is unchanged when the probability of employment equals $p(n)$ rather than $\bar{p}$, implying that at the margin the optimal family size will be larger.

The partial derivative $\partial E(w) / \partial n$ may be either positive or negative. If the following condition is satisfied, such that

$$(\partial p(n) / \partial n) \, f(l_w^c / n, s) + p(n) \, \partial f / \partial n > 0 \qquad (15)$$

then increasing the number of children in the family will increase the expected earnings of children. If n is increased, the effect on $E(W_c)$ is ambiguous because the probability of employment would rise but the average quality of children and hence the child's wage rate would decline. When n is increased, if factors influencing average quality do not vary much except below some minimum level of wife's time in child care activities, then the effect of the increased probability of employment dominates. In view of the previous discussion, when household economies of scale in the provision of minimal child care are present, the effect of the relatively minor decline in the child wage rate on expected child earnings is more than offset by the increased probability of family employment. The family would then choose not to practice family limitation.

Notes

Acknowledgments

1. The references to these papers are: "Child Labor in the Post-Bellum Southern Cotton Textile Industry," *Business and Economic History* 11 (1982): 136–146; "Earnings in the Post-Bellum Southern Cotton Textile Industry: A Case Study," *Exploration in Economic History* 21 (January 1984): 28–39; and "Schooling in the Post-Bellum Southern Cotton Mill Villages," *Journal of Social History* 20 (Fall 1986): 149–161.

Chapter 1

1. Herbert Gutman, *Work, Culture, and Society in Industrializing America: Essays in American Working Class and Social History* (New York: Vintage Books, 1977), p. 18.

2. Tamara K. Hareven, "The Family as Process: The Historical Study of the Family Cycle," *Journal of Social History* 7 (Spring 1974) and Hareven, *Family Time and Industrial Time: The Relationship between the Family and Work in a New England Industrial Community* (Cambridge: Cambridge University Press, 1982).

3. *American Museum,* July 1, 1970, Appendix IV, p. 2, Quoted in August Kohn, *The Cotton Mills of South Carolina* (Columbia: South Carolina Department of Agriculture, Commerce, and Immigration, 1907), p. 8.

4. *Mills' Statistics,* 1826, quoted in August Kohn, *The Cotton Mills of South Carolina* (Columbia: South Carolina Department of Agriculture, Commerce, and Immigration, 1907), p. 16.

5. Holland Thompson, *From the Cotton Field to the Cotton Mill: A Study of the Industrial Transition in North Carolina* (New York: Macmillan, 1906), p. 45.

6. Broadus Mitchell, *William Gregg: Factory Master of the Old South* (Chapel Hill: University of North Carolina Press, 1928), pp. 15–19.

7. Gavin Wright, *The Political Economy of the Cotton South: Households, Markets, and Wealth in the Nineteenth Century* (New York: W. W. Norton, 1978), p.94.

8. Broadus Mitchell, *The Rise of Cotton Mills in the South,* Johns Hopkins

University Studies in Historical and Political Science, vol. 39, no. 2 (Baltimore: Johns Hopkins Press, 1921), pp. 59–65.

9. Wilbur Joseph Cash, *The Mind of the South* (New York: Knopf, 1941; reprint ed., New York: Vintage Books, 1969), p. 180. Also, for a careful assessment of the importance of this movement, see David L. Carlton, *Mill and Town in South Carolina* (Baton Rouge: Louisiana State University Press, 1982), pp. 72–75.

10. Mitchell, *Rise of Cotton Mills,* p. 262; Melton Alonza McLaurin, *Paternalism and Protest: Southern Cotton Mill Workers and Organized Labor, 1875–1905,* Contributions in Economics and Economic History, no. 3 (Westport: Greenwood Press, 1971), p. 30; and U.S. Bureau of the Census, *Twelfth Census* (1900), vol. 9, *Manufactures: Special Reports on Selected Industries,* pt. 3 (Washington, D.C.: Government Printing Office, 1902): 29. Also see Alice Carol Galenson, *The Migration of the Cotton Textile Industry from New England to the South: 1880–1930* (New York: Garland Publishing, 1985), pp. 168–183.

11. Mitchell, *Rise of Cotton Mills,* p. 102.

12. W. F. Leake to Thomas Ruffin and his son-in-law Paul Cameron, 27 November 1868, Thomas Ruffin Papers, Southern Historical Collection, University of North Carolina Library, Chapel Hill, North Carolina.

13. W. F. Leake to Thomas Ruffin, 7 December 1868, Thomas Ruffin Papers, Southern Historical Collection, University of North Carolina Library, Chapel Hill, North Carolina.

14. Letter from son to his mother, mailed from Concord, North Carolina, 31 March 1889, Patterson Papers, North Carolina State Library and Archives, Raleigh, North Carolina.

15. Holland Thompson, *From the Cotton Field to the Cotton Mill,* pp.89–90.

16. Ibid., p. 89.

17. A mill treasurer, quoted in "Cotton Mills and the Commission Men," *Manufacturer's Report* 13 (March 3, 1888): 12.

18. David P. Doane, "Regional Cost Differentials and Textile Location: A Statistical Analysis," *Explorations in Economic History* 9 (Fall 1971): 3–34.

19. Galenson, *The Migration of the Cotton Textile Industry,* pp. 129–138.

20. H.R. Buist, quoted in Mitchell, *Rise of Cotton Mills,* p. 208.

21. For a discussion of the exclusion of blacks from most mill occupations, see Leonard A. Carlson, "Labor Supply, the Acquisition of Skills, and the Location of Southern Textile Mills, 1880–1900," *Journal of Economic History* 41 (March 1981): 70–71. Also, Daniel Nelson, *Managers and Workers: Origins of the New Factory System in the United States, 1880-1920* (Madison: University of Wisconsin Press, 1975), p. 90.

22. Andrew Warren Pierpont, "Development of the Textile Industry in Alamance County, North Carolina" (Ph.D. dissertation, University of North Carolina—Chapel Hill, 1953), pp. 33–45.

23. Edwin Michael Holt, Diary, 9 December 1845. Also, the entries from July–September, 1846, chronicled the progress of the dam and the water wheel expansion. Edwin Michael Holt Papers, Southern Historical Collection, University of North Carolina Library, Chapel Hill, North Carolina.

24. William Zachary at Holt's store to William A. Carrigan, 8 October 1847, John Warren Carrigan Papers, Manuscript Department, Duke University Lib-

rary, Durham, North Carolina. Also Edwin Michael Holt, Diary, 12 January 1848, proclaimed "All the Looms running." Edwin Michael Holt Papers, Southern Historical Collection, University of North Carolina Library, Chapel Hill, North Carolina.

25. Alfred A. Holt at Holt's store to William Holt, 8 May 1849, John Warren Carrigan Papers, Manuscript Department, Duke University Library, Durham, North Carolina.

26. Edwin Michael Holt, Diary, 3 September 1844 and 6 January 1847, quoted in Pierpont, "Development of the Textile Industry," p. 36.

27. Benson John Lossing, *Pictorial Field Book of the Revolution*, 2 vols. (New York: Harper & Brothers, 1860), 2: 38.

28. Letter from the Alamance Mill to Walter F. Carlile, 30 November 1902, Alamance Mill Papers, Southern Historical Collection, University of North Carolina Library, Chapel Hill, North Carolina.

29. Pierpont, "Development of the Textile Industry," pp. 170–171.

30. Morris Morris, *The Emergence of an Industrial Labor Force in India, A Study of the Bombay Cotton Mills, 1854–1947* (Berkeley: University of California Press, 1965), pp. 202, 210.

31. For example, H. J. Habakkuk analyzes the technological transformation of the economy induced by labor scarcity in *American and British Technology in the Nineteenth Century* (London: Cambridge University Press, 1962).

Chapter 2

1. Thomas F. Parker, president of Monaghan Mills, quoted in South Carolina Department of Agriculture, Commerce, and Immigration, *South Carolina: A Handbook* (Columbia: The State Company, 1908), p. 438.

2. Letter from son to his mother, Concord, North Carolina, 23 March 1891, Patterson Papers, North Carolina State Library and Archives, Raleigh, North Carolina.

3. Rental housing ledger for the Alamance Mill, Alamance Mill Papers, Southern Historical Collection, University of North Carolina Library, Chapel Hill, North Carolina. The sample of 348 textile operatives, which was collected by Gavin Wright and Cathy McHugh, is described in Appendix A.

4. A cotton manufacturer in Randolph County, North Carolina, quoted in North Carolina Bureau of Labor Statistics, *Annual Report,* 1887 (Raleigh: State Printer and Binder, 1887), p. 151.

5. Holland Thompson, *From the Cotton Field to the Cotton Mill: A Study of the Industrial Transition in North Carolina* (New York: Macmillan, 1906), p. 209; North Carolina Bureau of Labor Statistics, *Annual Report,* 1891 (Raleigh: State Printer and Binder, 1892), p. 128; and comments of a mill employee in Gaston County, North Carolina, quoted in North Carolina Bureau of Labor Statistics, *Annual Report,* 1887, p. 152.

6. Broadus Mitchell, *The Rise of Cotton Mills in the South,* Johns Hopkins University Studies in Historical and Political Science, vol. 39, no. 2 (Baltimore: Johns Hopkins Press, 1921), pp. 170–171.

7. Manager of a Cleveland County mill, quoted in North Carolina Bureau of Labor Statistics, *Annual Report,* 1891, p. 136.

8. T.S. Raworth, Augusta, Georgia, 30 December 1916, quoted in Mitchell, *Rise of Cotton Mills,* p. 171.

9. David L. Carlton, *Mill and Town in South Carolina,* 1880–1920 (Baton Rouge: Louisiana State University Press, 1982), pp. 91–95.

10. U.S. Commissioner of Labor, *Report on Condition of Woman and Child Wage-Earners,* Senate Document #645, 61st Cong., 2d sess., vol. 1 (Washington, D.C.: Government Printing Office, 1910): 570; Harriet L. Herring, *Welfare Work in Mill Villages: The Story of Extra Mill Activities in North Carolina* (Chapel Hill: University of North Carolina Press, 1929), p. 36.

11. North Carolina Bureau of Labor and Printing, *Annual Report,* 1903 (Raleigh: State Printer and Binder, 1904), pp. 111–112. Of 47 counties for which literacy rates of adult textile workers were available, 13 counties (28%) reported literacy rates greater than that of Alamance County. The reported literacy rates for adults ·by county ranged from 60% to 100%. Of 43 counties for which literacy rates of children were available, Alamance County ranked ninth.

12. Gerald W. Johnson, *The Making of a Southern Industrialist: A Biographical Study of Simpson Bobo Tanner,* quoted in Jack Blicksilver, *Cotton Manufacturing in the Southeast: An Historical Analysis* (Atlanta: Bureau of Business and Economic Research at Georgia State College of Business Administration, 1959), p.20.

13. U.S. Commissioner of Labor, *Report on Condition of Woman and Child Wage-Earners,* Senate Document #645, 61st Cong., 2d sess., vol. 17, *Hookworm Disease among Cotton-Mill Operatives* (Washington, D.C.: Government Printing Office, 1912): 23.

14. D. A. Rudisill of Cherryville Manufacturing Co., quoted in North Carolina Bureau of Labor and Printing, *Annual Report,* 1907 (Raleigh: State Printer and Binder, 1908), p. 248.

15. August Kohn, *The Cotton Mills of South Carolina,* p. 61, quoted in Blicksilver, *Cotton Manufacturing in the Southeast,* p. 36.

16. David P. Doane, "Regional Cost Differentials and Textile Location: A Statistical Analysis," *Explorations in Economic History* 9 (Fall 1971): 21.

17. Henderson Monroe Fowler, Diary, 12 January 1879 and April 1879, Henderson Monroe Fowler Papers, Southern Historical Collection, University of North Carolina Library, Chapel Hill, North Carolina.

18. Alan S. Blinder, "Wage Discrimination: Reduced Form and Structural Estimates," *Journal of Human Resources* 8 (Fall 1973): 437. For an elementary discussion of multiple regression analysis, see Ralph E. Beals, *Statistics for Economists* (Chicago: Rand McNally, 1972).

19. In addition to length of employment within Alamance Mill it may be desirable to consider an alternative measure of total work experience. One proxy for prior work experience is (age - 13 - experience), where 13 is considered the starting age of employment. However, inclusion of this variable in the regression model does not substantially improve the results. Perhaps total factory work experience would be a more relevant variable for consideration, but this information is not available.

20. A mill manager in Cleveland Co., quoted in North Carolina Bureau of Labor Statistics, *Annual Report,* 1891, p. 135.

21. Letter from son to mother, 14 November 1888, Patterson Papers, North

Carolina State Library and Archives, Raleigh, North Carolina.

22. Jacob Mincer, *Schooling, Experience, and Earnings* (New York: National Bureau of Economic Research, 1974).

23. Joanne Salop and Steven Salop, "Self-Selection and Turnover in the Labor Market," *Quarterly Journal of Economics* 90 (November 1976): 619–628.

24. According to Joanne Salop and Steven Salop, "Self-Selection" (p. 620), "the guarantee enables the firm to trust the applicant's protestations that he is a steady and stable worker, at the same time that it makes the firm relatively indifferent to the truth, since the firm no longer bears the onus of being wrong."

25. Unfortunately, the data do not allow us to distinguish clearly between the two effects. One possible test for determining the effects of experience on productivity would be to estimate the earnings functions for all piece-rate workers. The regression results for all piece-rate workers yield coefficients on experience that are generally positive. However, no strong conclusions may be drawn as the group of piece-rate workers is composed of two diverse subgroups: the weavers, with high mean wages and experience; and all other piece-rate workers with generally lower earnings and experience.

26. Claudia Goldin has empirically determined that when both men and women held jobs in the same occupations in the same manufacturing firms at the turn of the century, the method of remuneration tended to be payment by the piece in "Monitoring Costs and Occupational Segregation by Sex: An Historical Analysis," National Bureau of Economic Research Working Paper no. 1560 (February 1985), p. 13.

27. Gary Saxonhouse has discussed this effect within the Japanese textile industry in "Country Girls and Communication Among Competitors in the Japanese Cotton Spinning Industry," in *Japanese Industrialization and Its Social Consequences,* ed. Hugh Patrick (Berkeley: University of California Press, 1976), pp. 97–125.

28. The employment of many women may have influenced the method of payment as well as relative wages. Claudia Goldin in "Monitoring Costs," pp. 12–13, has found that in female-intensive industries, piece-rate payment systems were common.

29. The estimated coefficient on sex may exaggerate the effect of discrimination due to errors in variables or misspecification of the model. See Masanori Hashimoto and Levis Kochin, "A Bias in the Statistical Estimation of the Effects of Discrimination," *Economic Inquiry* 18 (July 1980): 478–486.

30. Blinder, "Wage Discrimination," pp. 436–455.

31. Ibid., pp. 438–439.

32. As a basis of comparision, a recent study of the wage difference between white married men and women in 1966 estimated that the wage gap equaled about 50% of the female wage rate. Correction for differences in work experience reduced the gap by one-fourth. The remaining unexplained portion of the wage gap could be interpreted as an upper bound of the effect of discrimination. Belton M. Fleisher and Thomas J. Kniesner, *Labor Economics: Theory, Evidence, and Policy,* 2d ed. (Englewood Cliffs: Prentice-Hall, 1980), pp. 352–353.

33. According to Claudia Goldin in "Monitoring Costs," if the tenure of

women employees is generally more limited in duration than the tenure of male employees, then a firm may tend to offer piece-rate payments to the women with greater frequency than to the males in order to minimize supervisory costs. In the Alamance Mill during the first week of January in 1890 and 1900, approximately two-thirds of the females were compensated on a piece-rate basis. In contrast, less than half of the males were paid by the piece.

34. Based on a much larger sample of females in the textile industry in 1907, Claudia Goldin and Donald Parsons have estimated that education tended to increase earnings approximately 2% per year due chiefly to gains from literacy. (They converted the variable months of school to a nine-month school year.) Claudia Goldin, "The Historical Evolution of Female Earnings Functions and Occupations," *Explorations in Economic History* 21 (January 1984): 6; and Claudia Goldin and Donald O. Parsons, "Economic Well-Being and Child Labor: The Interaction of Family and Industry," National Bureau of Economic Research Working Paper no. 707, p. 19.

Chapter 3

1. Felix Adler (founder of Ethical Culture Society and Chairman of National Child Labor Committee), speech in 1905, quoted in *Children and Youth in America: A Documentary History,* ed. by Robert H. Bremner, 3 vols. (Cambridge: Harvard University Press, 1971), 2: 653.

2. Edwin Markham, "The Hoe-Man in the Making: The Child at the Looms," *Cosmopolitan* 41 (August/September 1906): 482.

3. Holland Thompson, *From the Cotton Field to the Cotton Mill: A Study of the Industrial Transition in North Carolina* (New York: Macmillan, 1906), p. 244.

4. U.S. Bureau of the Census, *Thirteenth Census* (1909), vol. 10, *Manufactures: Reports for Principal Industries* (Washington, D.C.: Government Printing Office, 1913): 42.

5. A mill worker in Cleveland County, North Carolina, quoted in North Carolina Bureau of Labor Statistics, *Annual Report,* 1891 (Raleigh: State Printer and Binder, 1892), p. 171.

6. Dwight Ashley of Ashley Bailey Co., Fayetteville, North Carolina, quoted in North Carolina Bureau of Labor Statistics, *Annual Report,* 1905 (Raleigh: State Printer and Binder, 1905), p. 248.

7. J. M. Roberts, Secretary-Treasurer of John Rudisill Manufacturing Co., Lincolnton, North Carolina, quoted in North Carolina Bureau of Labor and Printing, *Annual Report,* 1907 (Raleigh: State Printer and Binder, 1908), p. 249.

8. W. Arthur Lewis, "Economic Development with Unlimited Supplies of Labor," *Manchester School* 22 (May 1954): 139–191.

9. U.S. Department of Commerce and Labor, *Bulletin of the Bureau of Labor,* no. 52, "Child Labor in the United States" (May 1904), p. 540.

10. Claudia Goldin and Donald O. Parsons, "Economic Well-Being and Child Labor: The Interaction of Family and Industry," National Bureau of Economic Research Working Paper no. 707, July 1981, p. 32. Their estimate derives from a simultaneous equation model of children's earnings and fathers' earnings. In their model they control for the influence of skill, age, regional wage levels, and nationality. See also Robert Hunter, *Poverty: Social Conscience in the Progressive*

Era (New York: Macmillan, 1917), c. 1904, pp. 245–246.

11. According to Alice Galenson, the labor supply function in the southern cotton textile industry was highly elastic. Alice Carol Galenson, *The Migration of the Cotton Textile Industry from New England to the South, 1880–1930* (New York: Garland Publishing, 1985), pp. 129–138. Further, the mill managers tended to increase recruiting and hiring expenditures to moderate wage increases.

12. A. G. Lineberger, quoted in North Carolina Bureau of Labor and Printing, *Annual Report,* 1905, p. 249.

13. J. W. Watts, Watts Manufacturing Co., Liledoun, North Carolina, quoted in North Carolina Bureau of Labor and Printing, *Annual Report,* 1907, p. 244.

14. Michael R. Haines, "Inequality and Childhood Mortality: A Comparison of England and Wales, 1911, and the United States, 1900," *Journal of Economic History* 45 (December 1985): 885.

15. U.S. Commissioner of Labor, *Report on Condition of Woman and Child Wage-Earners in the United States,* Senate Document #645, 61st Cong., 2d Sess., vol. 1 (Washington, D.C.: Government Printing Office, 1910): 365–366, 387.

16. U.S. Commissioner of Labor, *Report on Condition of Woman and Child Wage-Earners,* vol. 17, *Hookworm Disease among Cotton-Mill Operatives* (Washington, D.C.: Government Printing Office, 1912): 10–11.

17. Ibid., p. 21.

18. Mark Aldrich, "Determinants of Mortality Among New England Cotton Mill Workers During the Progressive Era," *Journal of Economic History* 42 (December 1982): 862, 855–856. Also, there is evidence of a correlation between health and skill level in English cotton textile factories, suggesting that only healthy workers were able to get and keep good jobs. Herman Freudenberger, Frances J. Mather, and Clark Nardinelli, "A New Look at the Early Factory Labor Force," *Journal of Economic History* 44 (December 1984): 1085–1090.

19. Haines, "Inequality and Childhood Mortality," p. 890. According to Jeffrey Williamson, infant mortality serves as a proxy for the disamenities of urban industrial life in "Was the Industrial Revolution Worth It? Disamenities and Death in 19th Century British Towns," *Explorations in Economic History* 19 (July 1982): 223.

20. Edgar Gardner Murphy, copy of manuscript of an unfinished book, *Issues: Southern and National,* Edgar Gardner Murphy Papers, Southern Historical Collection, University of North Carolina Library, Chapel Hill, North Carolina.

21. Thomas R. Dawley, Jr., "Our Mountain Problem and Its Solution," in American Cotton Manufacturers Association, *Proceedings of 14th Annual Convention* (Charlotte: 1910), p. 151.

22. A mill worker in Gaston County, North Carolina, quoted in North Carolina Bureau of Labor Statistics, *Annual Report,* 1887 (Raleigh: State Printer and Binder, 1887), p. 152.

23. Michael Reich, David M. Gordon, and Richard C. Edwards, "A Theory of Labor Market Segmentation," *American Economic Review* 63 (May 1973)· 359–365.

24. Harry M. Douty, cited by Andrew Warren Pierpont, "Development of the Textile Industry in Alamance County, North Carolina," (Ph.D. dissertation, University of North Carolina—Chapel Hill, 1953) p. 125.

25. North Carolina Bureau of Labor Statistics, *Annual Report,* 1891, p. 128.

26. Clem Moxley, a mill worker, quoted in Harriet Herring, *Welfare Work in Mill Villages: The Story of Extra Mill Activities in North Carolina* (Chapel Hill: University of North Carolina Press, 1929), p. 36.

27. U.S. Commissioner of Labor, *Woman and Child Wage-Earners,* 1: 63.

28. Morris Morris, "The Recruitment of an Industrial Labor Force in India, with British and American Comparisons," *Comparative Studies in Society and History* 2 (April 1960): 314–315.

29. For a discussion of the exclusion of blacks from most mill occupations, see Leonard A. Carlson, "Labor Supply, the Acquisition of Skills, and the Location of Southern Textile Mills, 1880–1900," *Journal of Economic History* 41 (March 1981): 70–71. Also Daniel Nelson, *Managers and Workers: Origins of the New Factory System in the United States, 1880–1920* (Madison: University of Wisconsin Press, 1975), p.90.

30. The following table provides the average daily wage for textile workers in North Carolina in 1887.

	Males	Females
Skilled	$1.65	$.65
Unskilled	.73	.41

Source: North Carolina Bureau of Labor Statistics, *Annual Report,* 1887, pp. 142–143.

31. For example, married women held no legal claim to their own earnings which were considered to be the absolute property of their husbands. Chief Justice Walter Clark, "The Legal Status of Women in North Carolina," copy of an address presented before the Federation of Women's Club, New Bern, North Carolina, 8 May 1913, Chief Justice Walter Clark Papers, North Carolina State Library and Archives, Raleigh, North Carolina.

32. A manager of Enterprise Manufacturing Co., Foust's Mills, North Carolina, quoted in North Carolina Bureau of Labor and Printing, *Annual Report,* 1903 (Raleigh: State Printer and Binder, 1904), p. 128.

33. A cotton mill operative in Randolph County, North Carolina, quoted in North Carolina Bureau of Labor Statistics, *Annual Report,* 1891, p. 178.

34. Manufacturer in Cabarrus County, North Carolina, quoted in North Carolina Bureau of Labor Statistics, *Annual Report,* 1887, p. 149.

35. Manufacturer in Alamance County, North Carolina, quoted in North Carolina Bureau of Labor Statistics, *Annual Report,* 1887, p. 148.

36. S. E. Bostick, superintendent of Worth Mill #3, Randleman, North Carolina, quoted in North Carolina Bureau of Labor and Printing, *Annual Report,* 1901 (Raleigh: State Printer and Binder, 1902), p. 220.

37. North Carolina Bureau of Labor and Printing, *Annual Report,* 1905, pp. 224–225, and *Annual Report,* 1907, pp. 218–219. See also Melvin Thomas Copeland, *The Cotton Manufacturing Industry of the United States* (Cambridge: Harvard University Press, 1912), pp. 143–144.

38. U.S. Bureau of the Census, *Thirteenth Census,* (1909), vol. 10, *Manufac-*

tures: Reports for Principal Industries: 42.

39. Manufacturer in Surry County, North Carolina, quoted in North Carolina Bureau of Labor Statistics, *Annual Report,* 1891, p. 153.

40. South Carolina mill poster, quoted in U.S. Department of Commerce and Labor, "Child Labor in the United States," pp. 491–492.

41. Gary Saxonhouse and Gavin Wright, "Two Forms of Cheap Labor in Textile History," in *Technique, Spirit and Form in the Making of the Modern Economies: Essays in Honor of William N. Parker,* ed. Saxonhouse and Wright, Research in Economic History, supplement 3 (Greenwich: JAI Press, Inc., 1984), p. 18. In comparison with the textile industry in New England, the southern mills hired proportionately fewer women and girls. This may be related to the relatively high productivity of females in southern agriculture. This topic is analyzed in Chapter 6. See Claudia Goldin and Kenneth Sokoloff, "The Relative Productivity Hypothesis of Industrialization: The American Case, 1820–1850," *Quarterly Journal of Economics* 99 (August 1984): 461–488.

42. Manufacturer in Guilford County, North Carolina, quoted in North Carolina Bureau of Labor Statistics, *Annual Report,* 1891, p. 141.

43. Manufacturer in Alamance County, North Carolina, quoted in North Carolina Bureau of Labor Statistics, *Annual Report,* 1887, p. 148.

44. H. F. Schenck, president of Cleveland Cotton Mills, Lawndale, North Carolina, quoted in North Carolina Bureau of Labor and Printing, *Annual Report,* 1903, p. 131.

45. Thompson, *From the Cotton Field to the Cotton Mill,* p. 189; and Wilbur Joseph Cash, *The Mind of the South* (New York: Knopf, 1941; reprinted ed., New York: Vintage Books, 1969), p. 250. For a study of the early attempts at labor organization, see Melton Alonza McLaurin, *Paternalism and Protest: Southern Cotton Mill Workers and Organized Labor, 1875-1905,* contributions in Economic History, no. 3 (Westport: Greenwood Press, 1971).

46. W. J. McLendon, Jr., Wadesboro Cotton Mills, Wadesboro, North Carolina, quoted in North Carolina Bureau of Labor and Printing, *Annual Report,* 1903, p. 140.

47. Conrad Taeuber and Irene B. Taeuber, *The Changing Population of the United States* (New York: John Wiley & Sons, 1958), p. 34.

48. For a thorough discussion of the controversy surrounding the legislative reform, see Elizabeth Davidson, *Child Labor Legislation in the Southern Textile States* (Chapel Hill: University of North Carolina Press, 1939). Also, Arden J. Lea, "Cotton Textiles and the Federal Child Labor Act of 1916," *Labor History* 16 (Fall 1975): 485-494.

49. Cash, *The Mind of the South,* pp. 216, 230.

50. H. F. Schenck, president of Cleveland Mill and Power Co., Lawndale, North Carolina, quoted in North Carolina Bureau of Labor and Printing, *Annual Report,* 1905, p. 247.

51. Paul Barringer, Tuscarora Cotton Mill, Mount Pleasant, North Carolina, quoted in North Carolina Bureau of Labor and Printing, *Annual Report,* 1903, p. 134.

52. D. A. Tompkins, manufacturer in Charlotte, North Carolina, quoted in North Carolina Bureau of Labor and Printing, *Annual Report,* 1901, p. 208.

53. Osborn Brown, president and superintendent of Long Island Cotton

Mills, Long Island, North Carolina, quoted in North Carolina Bureau of Labor and Printing, *Annual Report*, 1905, p. 246.

Chapter 4

1. Alexander J. Field, "Economic and Demographic Determinants of Educational Commitment, Massachusetts, 1855," *Journal of Economic History* 39 (June 1979): 439–457.

2. John Harrison Cook has argued that it was less costly for southern mills to finance mill schools than to pay municipal taxes for city services which included city schools in *A Study of the Mill Schools of North Carolina*, Contributions to Education, no. 178 (New York: Teachers College, Columbia University, 1925), p. 5.

3. U.S. Commissioner of Labor, *Report on Condition of Woman and Child Wage-Earners in the United States*, Senate Document #645, 61st Cong., 2d sess., vol. 1 (Washington, D.C.: Government Printing Office, 1910): 569, 571–572.

4. Harriet L. Herring, *Welfare Work in Mill Villages* (Chapel Hill: University of North Carolina Press, 1929), pp. 39–40.

5. North Carolina Bureau of Labor Statistics, *Annual Report*, 1890 (Raleigh: State Printer and Binder, 1890), p. 25.

6. Computed from data found in North Carolina Superintendent of Public Instruction, *Annual Report*, 1880 (Raleigh: State Printer and Binder, 1881), pp. 70–73. The classification of mill and nonmill counties was derived from the U.S. Bureau of the Census, *Tenth Census* (1880), vol. 2, *Statistics of Manufactures* (Washington, D.C.: Government Printing Office, 1883): 317–319. This difference is significant at the 95% confidence level.

7. Edgar Ralph Rankin, "A Social Study of One Hundred Families at Cotton Mills in Gastonia, North Carolina" (M.A. thesis, University of North Carolina—Chapel Hill, 1914), p. 24. However, with the gradual improvement in the quality of public schools, by 1920 many public schools may have been superior to mill schools. See David L. Carlton, *Mill and Town in South Carolina, 1880–1920* (Baton Rouge: Louisiana State University Press, 1982), pp. 96–100.

8. In contrast, Carlton emphasizes the role of public relations in explaining the provision of mill schools in *Mill and Town*, p. 93.

9. A. Michael Spence, *Market Signaling: Informational Transfer in Hiring and Related Screening Processes* (Cambridge: Harvard University Press, 1974).

10. Herring, *Welfare Work*, pp. 32–33.

11. Ibid., p. 33.

12. Gary Becker, *Human Capital*, 2d ed. (New York: National Bureau of Economic Research, 1975), pp. 36–37.

13. Housing ledger, Alamance Mill Papers, Southern Historical Collection, University of North Carolina Library, Chapel Hill, North Carolina.

14. Daniel Augustus Tompkins to Mrs. Charles A. Terry, 26 March 1913, Daniel Augustus Tompkins Papers, Manuscript Department, Duke University Library, Durham, North Carolina.

15. Finis Welch, "Education in Production," *Journal of Political Economy* 78 (January/February 1970): 35–39.

16. Melvin Thomas Copeland, *The Cotton Manufacturing Industry of the United*

States (Cambridge: Harvard University Press, 1912), p. 144.

17. Welch, "Education," pp. 35–39.

18. Alexander J. Field, "Educational Reform and Manufacturing Development in Mid-Nineteenth Century Massachusetts" (Ph.D. dissertation, University of California—Berkeley, 1974).

19. Herring, *Welfare Work,* p. 99.

20. William H. Williamson, President of Pilot Cotton Mills, Raleigh, North Carolina, quoted in North Carolina Bureau of Labor and Printing, *Annual Report,* 1907 (Raleigh: State Printer and Binder, 1908), p. 254.

21. J. A. Moore, Secretary of Harriet Mills, Henderson, North Carolina, quoted in Bureau of Labor and Printing, *Annual Report,* 1907, p. 253.

22. W. K. Parker, Cumberland, North Carolina, quoted in North Carolina Bureau of Labor Statistics, *Annual Report,* 1895 (Winston: Public Printers and Binders, 1895), p. 65.

23. "Courses of Study and Rules and Regulations of the Graded Schools of Reidsville," North Carolina, 1894–1895, pamphlet, p. 6.

24. A cotton textile manufacturer in Randolph County, North Carolina, quoted in North Carolina Bureau of Labor Statistics, *Annual Report,* 1891, p. 150.

25. "Suggestions and Test Questions for Review of Revised Course Study: 1901–1902," pamphlet, Johnston County Public Schools. Also, S. E. Bostick, Superintendent of Worth Mill, Randleman, North Carolina, quoted in North Carolina Bureau of Labor and Printing, *Annual Report,* 1901 (Raleigh: State Printer and Binder, 1902), p. 221.

26. Lincoln Cotton Mills manager, Southside, North Carolina, quoted in North Carolina Bureau of Labor and Printing, *Annual Report,* 1903 (Raleigh: State Printer and Binder, 1904), p. 139.

27. Samuel Bowles and Herbert Gintis, *Schooling in Capitalist America: Educational Reform and the Contradictions of Economic Life* (New York: Basic Books, 1976), p. 10.

28. Herbert J. Lahne, *The Cotton Mill Worker* (New York: Farrar & Rinehart, 1944). p. 63.

29. U.S. Commissioner of Labor, *Woman and Child Wage-Earners,* 1: 574.

30. Durham County Public Schools, *Annual Report,* 1902–1903 (Durham: Job Printer, 1903), pp. 3–27. This difference is significant at a 99% confidence level.

31. South Carolina Superintendent of Schools, *Annual Report,* 1905, p. 47. The relationship between school attendance and school quality has been analyzed by Susan Carter in "Occupational Segregation, Teachers' Wages, and American Economic Growth," *Journal of Economic History* 46 (June 1986): 374.

32. *The Annual Report of the Graded Schools of Morgantown, North Carolina for 1906–1907,* Bulletin # 7, (Raleigh: Edwards and Broughton, 1907), p. 21.

33. Rankin, "Social Study," p. 23.

34. Robert A. Margo considers the possibility that parental and child preferences regarding the schooling decision may differ in "Discussion," *Journal of Economic History* 42 (March 1982): 187.

35. Cotton mill operative, Cleveland County, North Carolina, quoted in North Carolina Bureau of Labor Statistics, *Annual Report,* 1891, p. 169.

36. William H. Watkins, Treasurer, Columbia Manufacturing Co., Ramseur,

North Carolina, quoted in North Carolina Bureau of Labor and Printing, *Annual Report,* 1903, p. 136.

37. Cotton mill worker, Cumberland County, North Carolina, quoted in North Carolina Bureau of Labor Statistics, *Annual Report,* 1891, p. 167.

38. South Carolina Superintendent of Schools, *Annual Report,* 1895, p. 7.

39. Beaming room worker, Randolph County, North Carolina quoted in North Carolina Bureau of Labor Statistics, *Annual Report,* 1891, p. 177; South Carolina Superintendent of Schools, *Annual Report,* 1905, p. 180; and U.S. Commissioner of Labor, *Woman and Child Wage-Earners,* 1: 574.

40. J. C. Reece, employee in Ramseur, Randolph County, North Carolina, quoted in North Carolina Bureau of Labor Statistics, *Annual Report,* 1896 (Winston: Public Printers and Binders, 1897), p. 81.

41. South Carolina Superintendent of Schools, *Annual Report,* 1905, p. 180.

42. Jennings J. Rhyne, *Some Southern Cotton Mill Workers and Their Villages* (Chapel Hill: University of North Carolina Press, 1930), pp. 158–159.

43. Harold Luft, "New England Textile Labor in the 1840s: From Yankee Farmgirl to Irish Immigrant," cited in Bowles and Gintis, *Schooling in Capitalist America,* p. 168; Thomas Dublin, *Women at Work: The Transformation of Work and Community in Lowell, Massachusetts, 1826–1860* (New York: Columbia University Press, 1979), pp. 150–151; and Claudia Goldin and Donald O. Parsons, "Economic Well-Being and Child Labor: The Interaction of Family and Industry," National Bureau of Economic Research Working Paper no. 707, July 1981, p. 19.

Chapter 5

1. Calvin B. Hoover and B. U. Ratchford, *Economic Resources and Policies of the South* (New York: Macmillan, 1951), p. 23.

2. Even as late as 1920, 80.9% of the population of North Carolina lived in rural areas. Of course, prior to the turn of the century the proportion was even greater. By 1938 in the Catawba Valley, a major textile area, 64% of the cotton yarn plants and 48% of the cotton fabric plants were located in towns with fewer than 10,000 residents. Rupert Vance, in collaboration with Nadia Danilevsky, *All These People: The Nation's Human Resources in the South* (Chapel Hill: University of North Carolina Press, 1945), p. 307.

3. Robert J. Willis, "A New Approach to the Economic Theory of Fertility Behavior," *Journal of Political Economy* 81 Supplement (March/April 1973): S14–S64.

4. For a discussion of the Massachusetts cotton mill communities, see Pamela Jean Nickless, "Changing Labor Productivity and the Utilization of Native Women Workers in the American Cotton Textile Industry, 1826–1860," (Ph.D. dissertation, Purdue University, 1976).

5. U.S. Commissioner of Labor, *Report on Condition of Woman and Child Wage-Earners in the United States,* Senate Document #645, 61st Congress, 2d sess., vol. 1 (Washington, D.C.: Government Printing Office, 1910): 770.

6. U.S. Bureau of the Census, Manuscript Census for Melville Township, Alamance County, North Carolina, 1900.

7. Dennis N. DeTray, "Child Quality and the Demand for Children," *Journal*

of Political Economy 81 Supplement (March/April 1973): S71.

8. See Claudia Goldin and Donald O. Parsons, "Economic Well-Being and Child Labor: The Interaction of Family and Industry," National Bureau of Economic Research Working Paper no. 707, July 1981. Goldin and Parsons observe an inverse relationship between school attendance by children of male textile workers and their father's earnings. This result suggests a negative correlation between the father's earnings and the probability that his children will work in the cotton mill.

9. U.S. Commissioner of Labor, *Women and Child Wage-Earners*, 1: 454, 460–461. This study left open the question of whether the father worked so little because many of his children were employed or vice versa.

10. For example, the 1900 Manuscript Census recorded farming as the usual occupation for a man who had been employed in the Alamance Mill for at least a year. Apparently he expected to return to farming as his primary occupation.

11. Dale Newman discusses the preference of management for hiring families with several girls in "Work and Community Life in a Southern Textile Town," *Labor History* 19 (Spring 1978): 205–206.

12. Letter from Alamance Mill manager to Mr. Hussey, Noise, North Carolina, 19 November 1906, Alamance Mill Papers, Southern Historical Collection, University of North Carolina Library, Chapel Hill, North Carolina.

13. A southern mill president, expressing concern over the early age of marriage within the mill villages stated that "There is also another proposed law which should receive attention, prohibiting the marriage of children, which are frequent in mill communities." Thomas F. Parker, quoted in South Carolina Department of Agriculture, Commerce, and Immigration, *South Carolina: A Handbook* (Columbia: The State Company, 1908), p. 438. Also, Holland Thompson, *From the Cotton Field to the Cotton Mill: A Study of the Industrial Transition* (New York: Macmillan, 1906), p. 167. Furthermore, southern women as a group perhaps tended to marry relatively early. A higher proportion of white women in North Carolina married before age 30 than in Massachusetts, as indicated by the following table.

Percentage of White Females Ever Married, by Age

	Percentage Ever Married	
Age	Massachusetts	North Carolina
15–19	5	16
20–24	35	56
25–29	59	78
30–34	72	86
35–39	78	89
40–44	82	90

Source: Computed from data in U.S. Bureau of the Census, *Sixteenth Census of the United States* (1940) *Population: Differential Fertility, 1940 and 1910: Fertility for States and Large Cities* (Washington, D.C.: Government Printing Office, 1943), pp. 150, 154.

14. U.S. Bureau of the Census, *Twelfth Census,* (1900), vol. 2, *Population,* part 2 (Washington: Government Printing Office, 1902): xci.

15. Ibid., pp. lxxxvii, lxxxix.

16. Ibid., p. lxxxix.

17. The estimation procedure and possible sources of bias are discussed in John Hajnal, "Age at Marriage and Proportions Marrying," *Population Studies* 7 (November 1953): 118–121, 126–131.

18. Roger L. Ransom and Richard Sutch, *One Kind of Freedom: The Economic Consequences of Emancipation* (New York: Cambridge University Press, 1977), p. 84. Further, August Kohn states that "The great majority of those who have gone to the cotton mills from farms belong to what is known as the tenant class." August Kohn, *The Cotton Mills of South Carolina* (Columbia: South Carolina Department of Agriculture, Commerce, and Immigration, 1907), p. 27.

19. This issue could be resolved in principle by comparing the age of marriage of mill workers with the age of marriage of tenant workers. These data are available in the 1900 Manuscript Census records.

20. U.S. Commissioner of Labor, *Woman and Child Wage-Earners,* 1: 436.

21. Clyde V. Kiser, "Trends in Annual Birth Rates Among Married Women in Selected Areas According to Nativity, Age, and Social Class," *Milbank Memorial Fund Quarterly Bulletin* 15 (January 1937): 48–74.

22. U.S. Commissioner of Labor, Seventh Annual Report, *Cost of Production: The Textiles and Glass,* vol. 2, part 2, "Cost of Living," House Document #2958, 52nd Congress, 2d. Sess. (Washington, D.C.: Government Printing Office, 1891): 876–877, 887–889. Infant mortality was thought to be higher in the South than in the North. Under these conditions, the implied fertility differential would be even greater.

23. Calculated from data in North Carolina Bureau of Labor Statistics, *Annual Report,* 1891 (Raleigh: State Printer and Binder, 1892), pp. 160–161. Because of the relatively high proportion of single-parent households, an average family size of 5.3 implies that $3.3 \le C \le 4.3$, where C = average number of children per family.

24. Paul C. Glick, "Family Trends in the United States, 1890–1940," *American Sociological Review* 7 (August 1942): 512.

25. U.S. Commissioner of Labor, *Woman and Child Wage-Earners,* 1: 413–414.

26. For a discussion of the role of slaveowners (employers) in fostering the pro-natal customs of the black slaves within the antebellum plantation community, see Herbert G. Gutman and Richard Sutch, "Victorians All? The Sexual Mores and Conduct of Slaves and Their Masters," in Paul David, Herbert G. Gutman, Richard Sutch, Peter Temin, and Gavin Wright, *Reckoning with Slavery: A Critical Study in the Quantitative History of American Negro Slavery* (New York: Oxford University Press, 1976), pp. 134–160.

27. Walter Richard Henry, "Cotton and the Commission Merchants," pamphlet (Raleigh: P. W. Wiley, 1883), p. 12.

28. Allison Davis, Burleigh Gardner, and Mary Gardner, *Deep South: A Social Anthropological Study of Caste and Class* (Chicago: University of Chicago Press, 1936), p. 127.

29. Vance, *All These People,* p. 105.

30. Ibid., p. 102. Unfortunately the data are not standardized for age at marriage.

Chapter 6

1. Thomas Dublin, *Women at Work: The Transformation of Work and Community in Lowell, Massachusetts, 1826–1860* (New York: Columbia University Press, 1979), pp. 26–27. There was a heavier reliance on child labor in the "Rhode Island Type" spinning mills than in the Lowell mills. However, by the mid-1830s, these mills were declining in importance in New England. The discussion here of New England mills is limited to consideration of the "Lowell type" mills.

2. Gary Saxonhouse, "The Supply of Quality Workers and the Demand for Quality in Jobs in Japan's Early Industrialization," *Explorations in Economic History* 15 (January 1978): 46.

3. Alexander Field, "Educational Reform and Manufacturing Development in Mid-Nineteenth Century Massachusetts," (Ph.D. dissertation, University of California—Berkeley, 1974), p. 184.

4. Dublin, *Women at Work*, pp. 33–34. There is a potential bias in Dublin's evidence. He tried to find the families of origin of the female mill workers. Those families whose incomes were really marginal were less likely to remain in the same location long enough to be found from census reports subsequent to the date at which the farm daughters were recorded on the mill payroll. Also, see Caroline F. Ware, *The Early New England Cotton Manufacture: A Study in Industrial Beginnings* (Boston: Houghton Mifflin, 1931), p. 217.

5. Massachusetts House Documents, 1845, no. 50, Appendix A, p. 20, quoted in Ware, *New England Cotton Manufacture*, p. 217.

6. Yukio Masui, "The Supply Price of Labor: Farm Family Workers," in *Agriculture and Economic Growth: Japan's Experience*, ed. by Kazushi Ohkawa, Bruce F. Johnston, and Hiromitsu Kaneda (Princeton: Princeton University Press, 1969), pp. 222–249.

7. Robert E. Cole and Ken'ichi Tominaga, "Japan's Changing Occupational Structure and Its Significance," in *Japanese Industrialization and Its Social Consequences*, ed. by Hugh Patrick (Berkeley: University of California Press, 1976), pp. 62, 56.

8. Claudia Goldin and Kenneth Sokoloff, "The Relative Productivity Hypothesis of Industrialization: The American Case, 1820–1850," *Quarterly Journal of Economics* 99 (August 1984): 483.

9. Manufacturer in Surry County, North Carolina, quoted in North Carolina Bureau of Labor Statistics, *Annual Report*, 1891 (Raleigh: State Printer and Binder, 1892), p. 153.

10. Saxonhouse, "Supply of Quality Workers," p. 66. Also, Gary R. Saxonhouse, "Country Girls and Communication Among Competitors in the Japanese Cotton-Spinning Industry," in *Japanese Industrialization and Its Social Consequences*, ed. by Hugh Patrick (Berkeley: University of California Press, 1976), pp. 99–125.

11. Saxonhouse, "Country Girls," pp. 101, 103.

12. Ibid., pp. 105–106.

13. Tamara K. Hareven, "The Family as Process: The Historical Study of the Family Cycle," *Journal of Social History* 7 (Spring 1974): 322-329.

14. Herbert Lahne, *The Cotton Mill Worker* (New York: Farrar & Rinehart, 1944), p. 66.

15. Dublin, *Women at Work*, p. 49.

16. Ibid., pp. 57, 50–55.

17. Cole and Tominaga, "Japan's Changing Occupational Structure," p. 59; Charles K. Moser, *The Cotton Textile Industry of Far Eastern Countries* (Boston: Pepperell Manufacturing, 1930), p. 18.

18. Morris Morris, *The Emergence of an Industrial Labor Force in India: A Study of the Bombay Cotton Mill, 1854–1947* (Berkeley: University of California Press, 1965), pp. 6, 203.

19. Lahne, *Cotton Mill Worker*, p. 6. Also, pp. 60, 63.

20. E. P. Thompson, *The Making of the English Working Class* (Harmondsworth: Penguin, 1968); Herbert Gutman, "Work, Culture, and Society in Industrializing America, 1815–1919," *American Historical Review* 78 (June 1973): 531–588; and Joan W. Scott and Louise A. Tilly, "Women's Work and the Family in Nineteenth Century Europe," *Comparative Studies in Society and History* 17 (January 1975): 36–64.

21. Wilbur Joseph Cash, *The Mind of the South* (New York: Knopf, 1941; reprint ed., New York: Vintage Books, 1969), p. 205.

22. Eugene Genovese, *Roll, Jordan, Roll: The World the Slaves Made* (New York: Pantheon Books, 1974), p. 4.

Selected Bibliography

Becker, Gary S. *Human Capital.* 2nd ed. New York: National Bureau of Economic Research, 1975.

Billings, Dwight B. *Planters and the Making of a "New South": Class, Politics, and Development in North Carolina, 1865–1900.* Chapel Hill: University of North Carolina Press, 1979.

Blicksilver, Jack. *Cotton Manufacturing in the Southeast: An Historical Analysis.* Atlanta: Bureau of Business and Economic Research, School of Business Administration, Georgia State College, 1959.

Blinder, Alan S. "Wage Discrimination: Reduced Form and Structural Estimates." *Journal of Human Resources* 8 (Fall 1973): 436–455.

Bowles, Samuel, and Gintis, Herbert. *Schooling in Capitalist America: Educational Reform and the Contradictions of Economic Life.* New York: Basic Books, 1976.

Carlson, Leonard A. "Labor Supply, the Acquisition of Skills, and the Location of Southern Textile Mills, 1880–1900." *Journal of Economic History* 61 (March 1981): 65–71.

Carlton, David L. *Mill and Town in South Carolina, 1880–1920.* Baton Rouge: Louisiana State University Press, 1982.

Cash, Wilbur Joseph. *The Mind of the South.* New York: Knopf, 1941; reprint ed., New York: Vintage Books, 1969.

Copeland, Melvin Thomas. *The Cotton Manufacturing Industry in the United States.* Cambridge: Harvard University Press, 1912.

David, Paul A. "Fortune, Risk, and the Microeconomics of Migration." In *Nations and Households in Economic Growth: Essays in Honor of Moses Abramovitz.* Edited by P. A. David and M. W. Reder. New York: Academic Press, 1974.

Davidson, Elizabeth H. *Child Labor Legislation in the Southern Textile States.* Chapel Hill: University of North Carolina Press, 1939.

Doane, David P. "Regional Cost Differentials and Textile Location: A Statistical Analysis." *Explorations in Economic History,* ser. 2, 9 (Fall 1971): 3–34.

Dublin, Thomas. *Women at Work: The Transformation of Work and Community in Lowell, Massachusetts, 1826–1860.* New York: Columbia University Press, 1979.

Field, Alexander. "Educational Reform and Manufacturing Development in Mid-Nineteenth Century Massachusetts." Ph.D. dissertation, University of California-Berkeley, 1974.

———. "Industrialization and Skill Intensity: The Case of Massachusetts." *Journal of Human Resources* 39 (Spring 1980): 149–175.

———. "Sectoral Shift in Antebellum Massachusetts: A Reconsideration." *Explorations in Economic History* 15 (April 1978): 146–171.

Fischbaum, Marvin Nelson. "An Economic Analysis of the Southern Capture of the Cotton Textile Industry Progressing to 1910." Ph.D. dissertation, Columbia University, 1965.

Galenson, Alice Carol. *The Migration of the Cotton Textile Industry from New England to the South, 1880–1930.* New York: Garland Publishing, 1985.

Genovese, Eugene. *In Red and Black: Marxian Explorations in Southern and Afro-American History.* New York: Pantheon Books, 1971.

Gilman, Glenn. *Human Relations in the Industrial Southeast: A Study of the Textile Industry.* Chapel Hill: University of North Carolina Press, 1956.

Goldin, Claudia, and Parsons, Donald O. "Economic Well-Being and Child Labor: The Interaction of Family and Industry." National Bureau of Economic Research Working Paper no. 707.

Grabill, Wilson H.; Kiser, Clyde V.; and Whelpton, Pascal K. *The Fertility of American Women.* New York: John Wiley & Sons, 1958.

Gutman, Herbert. *Work, Culture, and Society in Industrializing America: Essays in American Working Class and Social History.* New York: Vintage Books, 1977.

Habakkuk, Hrothgar John. *American and British Technology in the Nineteenth Century: The Search for Labour-Saving Inventions.* London: Cambridge University Press, 1962.

Hall, Jacquelyn Dowd; Korstad, Robert; and Leloudis, James. "Cotton Mill People: Work, Community, and Protest in the Textile South, 1880–1940." *American Historical Review* 91 (April 1986): 245–286.

Hareven, Tamara K. *Family Time and Industrial Time: The Relationship between the Family and Work in a New England Industrial Community.* Cambridge: Cambridge University Press, 1982.

Herring, Harriet L. *Southern Industry and Regional Development.* Chapel

Hill: University of North Carolina Press, 1940.

————. *Welfare Work in Mill Villages: The Story of Extra Mill Activities in North Carolina*. Chapel Hill: University of North Carolina Press, 1929.

Kiser, Clyde V. "Trends in Annual Birth Rates Among Married Women in Selected Areas According to Nativity, Age, and Social Class." *Milbank Memorial Fund Quarterly Bulletin* 15 (January 1937): 48–71.

Kohn, August. *The Cotton Mills of South Carolina*. Columbia: South Carolina Department of Agriculture, Commerce, and Immigration, 1907.

Lahne, Herbert J. *The Cotton Mill Worker in the Twentieth Century*. New York: Farrar & Rinehart, 1944.

Lemert, Benjamin Franklin. *Cotton Textile Industry of the Southern Appalachian Piedmont*. Chapel Hill: University of North Carolina Press, 1933.

McLaurin, Melton Alonza. *Paternalism and Protest: Southern Cotton Mill Workers and Organized Labor, 1875–1905*. Westport, Conn.: Greenwood Publishing Corporation, 1971.

Masui, Yukio. "The Supply Price of Labor: Farm Family Workers." In *Agriculture and Economic Growth: Japan's Experience*. Edited by Kazushi Ohkawa, Bruce F. Johnston, and Hiromitsu Kaneda. Tokyo: University of Tokyo Press, 1969.

Mitchell, Broadus. *The Rise of Cotton Mills in the South*. Johns Hopkins University Studies in Historical and Political Science, vol. 39, no. 8. Baltimore: Johns Hopkins Press, 1921.

Morris, Morris. *The Emergence of an Industrial Labor Force in India: A Study of the Bombay Cotton Mills, 1854–1947*. Berkeley: University of California Press, 1965.

Nelson, Daniel. *Managers and Workers: Origins of the New Factory System in the United States, 1880–1920*. Madison: University of Wisconsin Press, 1975.

Newman, Dale. "Work and Community Life in a Southern Town." *Labor History* 19 (Spring 1978): 204–225.

Nickless, Pamela Jean. "Changing Labor Productivity and the Utilization of Native Women Workers in the American Cotton Textile Industry, 1825–1860." Ph.D. dissertation, Purdue University, 1976.

Oates, Mary J. *The Role of the Cotton Textile Industry in the Economic Development of the American Southeast, 1900–1940*. New York: Arno Press, 1975.

Pencavel, John H. "Wages, Specific Training, and Labor Turnover in United States Manufacturing Industries." *International Economic*

Review 13 (February 1972): 53–64.

Pierpont, Andrew Warren. "Development of the Textile Industry in Alamance County, North Carolina." Ph.D. dissertation, University of North Carolina—Chapel Hill, 1953.

Potwin, Marjorie A. *Cotton Mill People of the Piedmont: A Study in Social Change.* New York: Columbia University Press, 1927.

Reich, Michael; Gordon, David M.; and Edwards, Richard C. "A Theory of Labor Market Segmentation." *American Economic Review* 68 (May 1973): 359–365.

Rhyne, Jennings J. *Some Southern Cotton Mill Workers and Their Villages.* Chapel Hill: University of North Carolina Press, 1930.

Salop, Joanne, and Salop, Steven. "Self-Selection and Turnover in the Labor Market." *Quarterly Journal of Economics* 90 (November 1976): 619–628.

Sandberg, Lars G. "American Rings and English Mules: The Role of Economic Rationality." *Quarterly Journal of Economics* 83 (February 1969): 25–43.

Saxonhouse, Gary R. "Country Girls and Communication Among Competitors in the Japanese Cotton-Spinning Industry." In *Japanese Industrialization and Its Social Consequences.* Edited by Hugh Patrick. Berkeley: University of California Press, 1976.

————. "The Supply of Quality Workers and the Demand for Quality in Jobs in Japan's Early Industrialization." *Explorations in Economic History* 15 (January 1978): 40–68.

Saxonhouse, Gary, and Wright, Gavin. "Two Forms of Cheap Labor in Textile History." In *Technique, Spirit and Form in the Making of the Modern Economies: Essays in Honor of William N. Parker,* pp. 3–31. Edited by Gary Saxonhouse and Gavin Wright. Greenwich, Conn.: JAI Press, 1984.

Scott, Joan W., and Tilly, Louise A. "Women's Work and the Family in Nineteenth Century Europe." *Comparative Studies in Society and History* 17 (January 1975): 36–64.

Smith, Robert Sidney. *Mill on the Dan: A History of Dan River Mills, 1882–1950.* Durham: Duke University Press, 1960.

Spence, Andrew Michael. *Market Signaling: Informational Transfer in Hiring and Related Screening Processes.* Cambridge: Harvard University Press, 1974.

Terrill, Tom E. "Murder in Graniteville." In *Toward a New South? Studies in Post-Civil War Southern Communities,* pp. 193–222. Edited by Orville Vernon Burton and Robert C. McMath, Jr. Westport: Greenwood Press, 1982.

Thompson, E. P. *The Making of the English Working Class.* Harmondsworth: Penguin, 1968.

Thompson, Holland. *From the Cotton Field to the Cotton Mill: A Study of the Industrial Transition in North Carolina.* New York: Macmillan, 1906.

Willis, Robert. "A New Approach to the Economic Theory of Fertility Behavior." *Journal of Political Economy* 81 Supplement (March/April 1973): 514–564.

Wright, Gavin. "Cheap Labor and Southern Textiles Before 1880." *Journal of Economic History* 39 (September 1979): 655–680.

————. "Cheap Labor and Southern Textiles, 1880–1930." *Quarterly Journal of Economics* 96 (Novermber 1981): 605–629.

————. *Old South, New South.* New York: Basic Books, 1986.

Index